Trading with CHART PATTERN *and* PRICE ACTION BREAKOUT

Trading with
CHART PATTERN
and
PRICE ACTION BREAKOUT

MAHESH CHANDRA KAUSHIK

PRABHAT
PRAKASHAN

Published by
PRABHAT PRAKASHAN PVT. LTD.
4/19 Asaf Ali Road,
New Delhi-110002 (INDIA)
e-mail: prabhatbooks@gmail.com

ISBN 978-93-5562-775-9

TRADING WITH CHART PATTERN AND PRICE ACTION BREAKOUT
by Mahesh Chandra Kaushik

Edition
First, 2025

Price
₹ 400 (Rupees Four Hundred Only)

Printed at
Sita Fine Arts, Delhi

Author's Note

My Dear Readers,

The world is moving forward very fast in the present times. Today's time can be called the fastest moving era till date.

The movies of the olden times were so slow and those of today are so fast! Now people do not like to watch a three-hour movie, because there is a rush everywhere in life. People have everything else, but have less time. That is why instead of a three-hour long movie, first came the era of a one-hour telefilm, then came the era of a 20-minute serial and now a person enjoys 60-second short videos (reels) as much as a movie.

This era of fast time is also showing its effect on people's investment in the share market. In the earlier slow time, people used to buy shares and hold them for 5-10-15-20-25 years.

Such investors used to earn dividends during holding and if the company whose shares were owned did well, they would become millionaires with the shares of their holdings. Even today, there are many such old- timers. A reel of an old man from Karnataka went viral in which he told how he had bought shares of UltraTech, Larsen & Toubro, and Karnataka Bank in his youth, which are worth more than ₹ 10 crores today and he gets dividends of lakhs of rupees annually.

However, today's people do not have that much patience. They buy shares in the morning and check in the evening itself to see how much per cent they have increased or decreased.

Today's investor does not want to earn returns by holding shares for a long term. He wants to earn returns by holding shares for just 1 day to 15 days by doing intraday trading or swing trading based on the price action.

This is so because today's investor is educated and intelligent. He knows the compounding principle of mathematics that if he invests ₹ 20,000 in a trade and gets 6 per cent profit in that trade, then next time, he adds ₹ 1,200 of this 6 per cent profit back to the principal amount and takes a trade of 21,200 and again books 6 per cent profit and adds it back to the principal amount and takes a trade of 22,472 next time, in this way, by doing this 108 times only, his rupees 20,000 will become rupees 1,00,00,000. Those who are not convinced can check this calculation using an excel sheet or calculator.

Now, how to earn 6 per cent on every trade? This is a tough question. It is as difficult as it looks easy and also as easy as it looks difficult.

Now you will say, Sir, do not confuse me by talking in circles! What do you want to say? Is it difficult or easy to earn 6 per cent on every trade?

If you are new, then look at some past data of the stock market to learn the answer to this question. You will see that many stocks enter the upper circuit by rising more than 6 per cent in a single day, i.e., by 10-15-20 per cent, and in many stocks, the reverse also happens, i.e., they do not rise by 6 per cent, but also fall on the contrary.

Everything depends on the fact that if a stock is going to rise by 5-10-15-20 per cent, you can identify from its movement whether it is going to rise or fall.

This is called 'Price Action Movement'. Just like the darkness of the night starts to disappear in the morning's *Brahma Muhurta* (the time of the Creator) before the sun rises, and the sky turns red, which gives the feeling that the sun is about to rise, so it happens with stocks in the share market. The stock which is about to rise, starts giving positive signals on the chart a few days before on the basis of its price movement. The sun turns red again at the time of sunset, birds start returning to their nests, the sky becomes hazy due to the dust raised by the feet of animals returning home and the pollution caused by the vehicles throughout the day; this is called 'Godhuli Vela' in Hindi. From that twilight, we get the feeling that the sun is setting. Similarly, even before the stock falls, we start getting some negative signals in the chart pattern. So if you learn to read these signals, the door to success may open for you and you may find it very easy to earn 6 per cent return in one trade.

These things may be a little difficult for a new trader to understand; but those who are old and experienced like me and are reading my book, should put their hand on their heart and ask whether they have not earned more than 6 per cent profit 108 times, let alone more than that, till date?

Then why could you not become a millionaire? The simple answer to this is that firstly, you did not know the rule of compounding, and secondly, you fell into the trap of the so-called chart experts and kept booking losses with stop losses along with profits, due to which you brought the boat back as much (sometimes even more) as you took it forward. Altogether, you are standing in the same place in the middle of the sea.

Then, while standing in the middle, you sing the song, "I would have got the support of some research analyst; if the storm had not come, I would have reached the shore." In Rajendra Kumar and Sadhana's song from the 1971 film, 'Aap Aaye Bahar Aayi', which was sung by Lata Mangeshkar and Mohammed Rafi—"I would have got the support of your love; if the storm had not come, I would have reached the shore" —I have used 'research analyst' instead of 'love'. (If you want, you can listen to this song on YouTube, shed some tears for a while and then read the book further.)

Before you start to read the book, I would like to make you take one more important oath, that is, "I swear that keeping aside all the knowledge of technical analysis that I have acquired till now, I will read this book thoroughly and with an impartial and open mind, without skipping even a single page".

Actually, I felt the need to make you take this oath because I know that most of the people buy any book, but after that, they do not have enough patience to read it.

Nowadays, people's ability to concentrate is decreasing due to watching short video statuses and reels and after reading a book for 30 seconds, they leave the text incomplete as per their habit and start reading from ahead by turning the pages, so that if there is some magical shortcut of 30 seconds mentioned in the book, then by reading that, they can become a master in trading quickly.

I do not want to disappoint you, but if you want to succeed in trading, then there is no shortcut for it. No matter how big this book seems to you, you will have to read it completely.

I have a valuable suggestion for you that the supreme power (whom you know by any name like Ishwar, Allah, God, Wahe Guru etc.) who has made me write this book as a medium has also selected you as the reader of this book.

Therefore, you should consider it a holy coincidence that this book has come into your hands. Therefore, do not consider it an ordinary book but a holy book and read it with full faith and respect, understand each page of it and absorb it. You may read only one or two pages daily, but do not move ahead without fully absorbing whatever you read.

After first expressing my gratitude to the Almighty God, I also express my gratitude to my Guruji, Late Shri-Shri 1008 Satyanarayan Dasji Falahari Baba, due to whose spiritual knowledge I was able to uplift my soul as well as make the lives of lakhs of people financially prosperous.

I am also thankful to most venerable Shri Sahdev Guruji Maharaj Naga Sannyasi, who helped me to overcome the absence of a Guru in my life after my Guruji departed to heaven. I am also thankful to my wife, Mrs Seema Kaushik (who also has a cooking channel on YouTube named 'Seema Ki Rasoi') that she never stopped me from trading in the stock market and always encouraged me.

I request the readers of the book to please not ask for my mobile number and call me to seek guidance, because it is not possible to talk to everyone on mobile due to having more than 6 lakh followers on YouTube.

Please also do not try to meet me at my home or at my workplace without informing me, because due to this, I would be unable to dedicate my time to my personal and official work. Those who want an informal meeting with me should stay in touch with the community posts of my YouTube channel. Whenever I come to any town, I inform about my arrival in a public park on the YouTube community post and my fans from nearby areas can meet me informally there. The videos of my recent meeting with my followers in Jodhpur and Hisar are also available on YouTube.

You can email me your views at mahesh2073@yahoo.com. Though it is not possible to reply to all emails, I try to reply to as many emails as I can.

—**Mahesh Chandra Kaushik**
Assistant Revenue Accountant,
SEBI Registered Research Analyst
Pindwara, District Sirohi, Rajasthan-307022

Contents

1

What are Candlestick Charts?

In December 1989, there was a trader in America named Steven Nison, who wrote a seminal article on candlestick chart patterns. Reading that article created a stir among the American traders because it explained the secret technique of earning profit from the market of Japanese traders.

In fact, Japanese traders were mostly in the winning position in the stock market of America at that time. Their predictions about the market were often correct. Seeing this, American traders were in a dilemma as to what kind of technique do the Japanese have by which they are able to predict the market so accurately? Later, America's Merrill Lynch Company published a booklet of Japanese charting technique told by Steven Nison, more than 10,000 copies of which were sold in a very short time.

Actually, in 1987, Steve Nison went to the office of a female Japanese broker. There she was making some candle-like shapes and pronouncing some Japanese words, such as Doji, Dark Cloud Cover, etc. From that, Steve Nison realised for the first time that it is through those candle-like shapes that Japanese people are able to accurately predict the direction of the market.

I appreciate Steve Nison's intelligence. If it had been a simpleton instead of him, he would have thought that they are doing some voodoo, tantric or black magic by making candles and reciting mantras in Japanese language, and that is why they are always able to earn from the stock market; and maybe, he would have been so scared that he would never have gone to that Japanese broker again.

After this, his interest grew in doing more research about candlestick chart patterns and he studied many books written in Japanese language on candlestick chart patterns with the help of Japanese to English translators at that time. Overall, I want to explain to you that Steve Nison was the first person who brought the Japanese knowledge of candlestick chart patterns before the world.

Now the question may be coming to your mind as to why this Japanese method is used all over the world to understand chart patterns. Let me first tell you about the history of this technical analysis.

Do you know who is known as 'The God of Markets?' You may have been trading in the market for 10-20 years, yet you may have never heard of 'The God of Markets'.

It is like someone studying a religious book and following the principles of a religion, but not knowing who the God of that religion is!

Today, first of all, let me introduce you to 'The God of Markets'. Actually, in the year 1724, a rice businessman named Munehisa Honma was born in Sakata city of Japan.

Munehisa Honma is also known by his other name, 'Sokyu Honma'.

The world's first future market was started in Japan during 1710, in which future prices of rice were traded through coupons. From that time, Sokyu Honma was a rice trader. By trading in rice, he earned so much money by 1755, which was equivalent to 10 billion dollars today.

Therefore, till date, there has been no successful trader like Munehisa Honma in history. This is the reason why he is also known in history as 'The God of Markets'.

Now, you must be wondering what this story has to do with you.

In fact, Munehisa Honma had written a book for traders in Japanese language in 1755, titled 'San-en-Kinsen'. Its English translation is also known as 'The Fountain of Gold—The Three Monkey Record of Money'.

The principles described by Munehisa Honma in this book later became the basis of candlestick charting.

You will be surprised to know that Sokyu Honma has not mentioned candlestick chart anywhere in this book. However, in candlestick charts, we basically predict the market movement from the psychology of the market. Understanding the psychology of the market is the basic key to technical analysis techniques around the world.

What is technical analysis? In technical analysis, we predict the direction of the market by reading the behaviour of traders from chart patterns, which is accurate up to 80 to 90 per cent.

Actually, technical analysis or chart pattern reading or price action breakout is the language of the market. When you learn this language, the market itself will tell you whether it is going to fall or rise. If you have bought this book, then you just have to keep one thing in mind that I have spent 1 year and 6 months of my life in writing this book.

Therefore, it is your duty to spend at least 3 to 7 days in reading this book completely. Do not keep it unread and do not skip reading in between.

If you want to read and learn the language of the market then you will have to imbibe the facts given in each chapter of the book along with me. Then this stock market itself will speak to you, talk to you and will be able to tell you all its secrets.

In this book, I will explain to you absolutely new techniques with practical examples. You will also have to practise a little yourself as I tell you. Then you will easily learn to create and read chart patterns without using chart software.

Now you must be thinking that when Sokyu Honma has not mentioned candlestick charts anywhere in his book, then why do we consider him the 'founder of candlestick chart pattern'?

Actually, he has explained the rules related to market behaviour in his book, 'The Fountain of Gold - The Three Monkey Record of Money'. This psychology of the market became the basis of candlestick chart pattern and only Japanese people used this type of candlestick chart, that is why Munehisa Honma's name is associated with candlestick chart. But in reality, the Japanese invented the candlestick chart in the late nineteenth century using the methods of Munehisa Honma.

Munehisa Honma has five major rules of technical analysis, which we will also use in the upcoming chapters.

Does the psychological behaviour of traders play an important role in the increase or decrease in the price of shares in the market?

You must have experienced many times that the market behaviour reacts less to fundamentals and more to local events. For example, during the outbreak of Corona in the year 2020, the prices of shares fell rapidly all over the world.

For example, the price of SBI, which is India's largest bank, was ₹ 370.65 on 5th July, 2019. It fell to just ₹ 166.40 on 15th May, 2020, when Corona arrived. But even at that price, most investors were not ready to buy it. They felt that due to Corona, it would be difficult for the country's economy to get back on track. Four years later, at the time of writing this book, when the market is in a bull run, the shares of the same SBI are looking cheap to people even at the price of 859.95.

You must have experienced this behaviour many times, like the stock market falls during elections.

I remember a funny incident of 1998. In 1998, when the US President, Bill Clinton, had an affair with his White House employee, Monica Lewinsky, the stock markets all over the world fell.

Now think for yourself, the fall in the market had nothing to do with the fundamentals of the shares and what link can the affair between Bill Clinton and Monica Lewinsky have with the stock market? You will find this funny!

But the market behaves psychologically like this. In India, wheat is mainly produced in Punjab, Haryana, Rajasthan and Madhya Pradesh. Once there was a famine and the prices of wheat were skyrocketing. At the same time, it rained in Mumbai, which is not a major wheat producing area. However, the news of rain in Mumbai brought down the prices of wheat across the country.

So, by understanding the psychological behaviour of investors from chart patterns, you can predict the market trend.

Most of my readers are intelligent and logical people, so I understand the question in their mind.

My readers will ask that the fall in the market due to such events is temporary, which lasts only from 1-2 days to 15-20 days. Then how can this help us in understanding the long-term behaviour of the market?

The answer to this question is that the bullish and bearish phase of the market is also purely based on the mental state of the investors.

In Japanese language, bull market is called 'Yang' and bear market is called 'Yin'. In fact, when there is a bull market or when any stock rises, you must have noticed that the market or that stock mostly keeps rising; that is, the stock which is rising keeps rising even when you wait for it to fall.

This happens due to the psychology of investors, because the rising stock looks good to everyone and more traders want to take a position in it, which increases the demand.

On the other hand, the investor who has such rising shares gets greedy and waits for the stock to rise a little more and then book profit. Due to this reason, he does not sell the shares in the rising market. Due to this mentality, the supply decreases.

Therefore, due to increased demand and reduced supply, such a stock makes new highs every day. This is the reason why you see that often, the rising stock keeps rising.

On the other hand, when a bear market comes or a bear phase comes in a stock, the investor sees that the mutual fund/stock in which he was making 45-50per cent profit till yesterday has come down to 30-35 per cent.

Now, the investor thinks that it does not matter since he has to stay long term. The market will rise again. But if the fall continues, then the next day his profit remains only 20-25 . Now he thinks that half of his profit has been wiped out, and if he waits any longer, his entire profit will be lost; so he also comes to sell the shares. On the other hand, investors willing to buy in a falling market feel that the fall in the market will increase further, so they should not buy now. Thus, in a falling market, supply increases and demand decreases.

In a falling market, people's stop losses also get triggered; hence, the supply increases. In a downtrend, people's mind-set shifts away from buying. They want to somehow book their profits and exit or want to sell to limit their losses.

This is the reason that in a falling market, due to increased selling and decreased buying, a falling market or stock always keeps falling. But always remember that day comes after night and night comes after day.

Similarly, the nature of market is also cyclical. In a bull market, the possibility of a bear market is hidden and in a bear market, the possibility of a bull market is always hidden.

Therefore, in chart patterns, you should understand the relationship of stock price with time by keeping in mind this first rule of Sokyu Honma.

You must have heard about the Gann method. In that too, emphasis is given on the ratio of time price.

In Darvas Box theory also, we take trades according to the weekly high level. Therefore, the first rule says that if you feel that the psychological effect of an event is of one day, then you should look at the chart of one day. If you see a five-day effect, then you should look at a five-day chart.

If you feel that the price of a stock fluctuates in a one-month cycle, then you should look at a one-month chart.

As of now, in Nifty and Bank Nifty, future contracts have weekly expiry, so it is better to look at their weekly charts and in shares, future contracts have monthly expiry, so it is better to read their monthly charts. You will be told about this in the subsequent chapters of this book.

2. Buy on a fall and sell on a rise—how simple is this rule! Even the most foolish man knows this simple principle of trading to buy on a fall and sell on a rise.

But it is very difficult to follow this principle practically. To understand this, listen to the story of my friend Haruka (name changed).

Haruka was my friend and was earning a lot of money in the property business; but in 2007, he was attracted by the boom in the market and started investing in the stock market. I was also new to the market at that time. The only difference was that I had entered the market around 2004 and Haruka had entered the market at the end of 2007.

Haruka thought that the price of shares fluctuates by 2 to 5 per cent every day, so money can be easily made by selling a share of ₹ 100 at ₹ 105. At that time, the market was in a bull run, so Haruka's bets started turning out to be correct. He would buy any share as soon as it fell a little and easily earn 5-6 per cent in a few days.

Haruka felt that this business was more interesting than investing in property, so he sold some plots and invested about ₹ 20 lakh in the market.

After that, in the year 2008, there was a big fall in the market and the Sensex fell from 20,645 to 9,716. In February 2009, it came down to just 8,891.

Haruka had not bought shares of good companies either, so his portfolio of ₹ 20 lakhs got reduced to ₹ 5 lakhs. So, after waiting for 1-2 years for the shares to grow, Haruka got fed up, booked a loss of ₹ 15 lakhs and said goodbye to the market forever.

Now why did Haruka lose ₹ 15 lakhs when he had followed the simple rule of Munehisa Honma to buy in the dip and sell in the uptrend?

In fact, Haruka only followed the above rule no. 2, so he suffered such a huge loss. As I have already told you, Sokyu Honma has five main rules, the third of which is as follows –

3. Sell at every substantial Koku drop from the top and buy at every substantial Koku rise from the bottom.

Now after reading this third rule, most of the readers must have got confused as to what is this Koku? Actually, Koku is the unit of measuring rice in Japan. Koku was a drum- like container, in which rice was packed and then transported. The volume of that drum- like cylindrical container called Koku was 180 litres from inside, which could hold about 150 kg of rice.

Now you must be thinking that if there was a rule to sell after a fall of so many per cent from the top or a rise of so many per cent from the bottom, then it would have been fine, but what does it mean to sell or buy after a fall of so many kilograms or a rise of so many kilograms?

Actually, here no importance has been given to the fall or rise in price; here the rule of trading has been given after a fall or rise in volume. That is why the word 'koku' has been used here, which is a unit of measuring volume.

At the time when these rules were initially written by Munehisa Honma, it was the year 1755. At that time, the markets were purely based on demand and supply, that is, if the volume of rice was high, then naturally the supply would increase and due to low demand, the prices would fall.

The markets of that time were the simplest form of market based on demand and supply. In such markets, the direction of trading in the market could be easily decided on the basis of increase or decrease in trading volume (rice koku).

In today's markets, computer-based trading takes place. Nowadays, the time of Kali Yuga is also at its peak, where Kali Yugi operators manipulate the volume so much by resorting to insider trading etc. in the market that a common innocent retailer cannot guess whether a stock will rise or fall on the basis of volume alone.

To explain this fact in detail, I have taken a screenshot on 2nd August, 2024 of 7 days volume and price data of Reliance Industries Limited share on NSE from 25th July, 2024 to 2nd August, 2024, which you can see in the below image.

Now, what would happen if you had estimated the market trade based on the increase or decrease in volume in this?

You can see that 62,59,938 shares were traded on 25th July, 2024 and 49,29,970 shares were traded on 26th July, 2024, that is, between 25th and 26th July, the volume fell significantly; but the price of the shares increased from 2,984.80 to close at 3,018.05. Now if someone thought that since the volumes fell on 25th and 26th July, the price will also fall in the trade of 27th July, then he would have been wrong. On 27th July, the volume was only 37,69,275 shares, but the price increased and closed at 3,040.20.

Thus, you can see in the above figure that generally there is no direct relationship between price and volume. When volumes are falling, sometimes price is rising, sometimes it is falling. Similarly, when volumes are rising, sometimes price is falling, sometimes it is rising.

What I mean to say is that we cannot make a position directly on the basis of rising or falling volumes.

4. If your trading prediction is wrong, then accept your mistake and get away from the market once.

To understand this rule, if you know any trader who has been ruined in the stock market, then listen to his story of ruin. If not, then listen to the stories of one or two ruined traders on YouTube.

Traders link their decisions in the stock market with their ego. After that, when their decision proves to be wrong, their ego does not accept it and instead of closing the position, they start insisting on making profit by averaging it. Even then, if they do not make any profit, they become more stubborn and start fighting the market and start increasing the position size. In doing this, when their entire capital is wiped out, then they come to their senses.

So, the gist of this rule is that if your prediction turns out to be wrong, close the position with a small loss and then take a break from

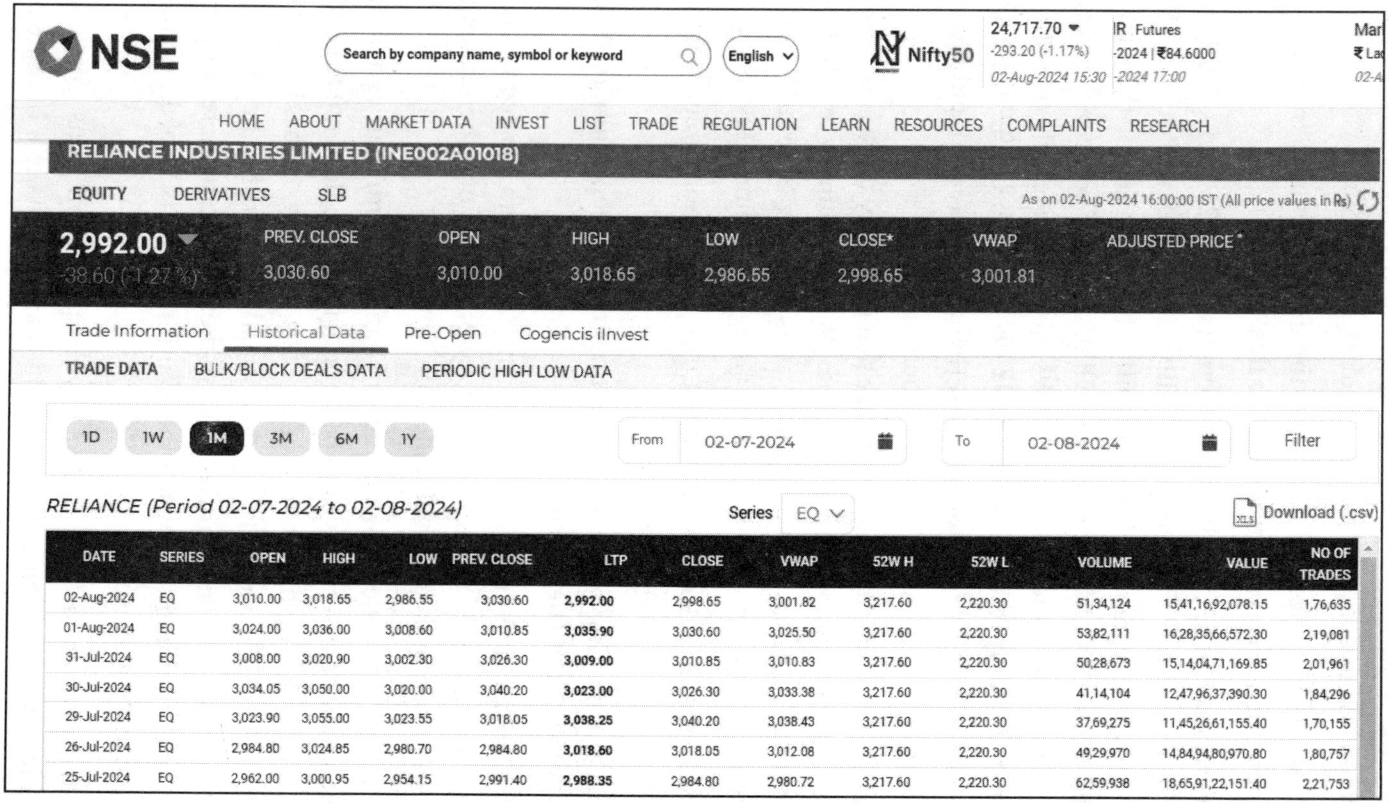

NSE | Search by company name, symbol or keyword | English | Nifty50 24,717.70 -293.20 (-1.17%) 02-Aug-2024 15:30 | IR Futures -2024 | ₹84.6000 -2024 17:00

HOME ABOUT MARKET DATA INVEST LIST TRADE REGULATION LEARN RESOURCES COMPLAINTS RESEARCH

RELIANCE INDUSTRIES LIMITED (INE002A01018)

EQUITY DERIVATIVES SLB

As on 02-Aug-2024 16:00:00 IST (All price values in Rs)

2,992.00	PREV. CLOSE	OPEN	HIGH	LOW	CLOSE*	VWAP	ADJUSTED PRICE*
-38.60 (-1.27 %)	3,030.60	3,010.00	3,018.65	2,986.55	2,998.65	3,001.81	-

Trade Information | Historical Data | Pre-Open | Cogencis iInvest

TRADE DATA | BULK/BLOCK DEALS DATA | PERIODIC HIGH LOW DATA

1D 1W 1M 3M 6M 1Y | From 02-07-2024 | To 02-08-2024 | Filter

RELIANCE (Period 02-07-2024 to 02-08-2024) Series EQ Download (.csv)

DATE	SERIES	OPEN	HIGH	LOW	PREV. CLOSE	LTP	CLOSE	VWAP	52W H	52W L	VOLUME	VALUE	NO OF TRADES
02-Aug-2024	EQ	3,010.00	3,018.65	2,986.55	3,030.60	**2,992.00**	2,998.65	3,001.82	3,217.60	2,220.30	51,34,124	15,41,16,92,078.15	1,76,635
01-Aug-2024	EQ	3,024.00	3,036.00	3,008.60	3,010.85	**3,035.90**	3,030.60	3,025.50	3,217.60	2,220.30	53,82,111	16,28,35,66,572.30	2,19,081
31-Jul-2024	EQ	3,008.00	3,020.90	3,002.30	3,026.30	**3,009.00**	3,010.85	3,010.83	3,217.60	2,220.30	50,28,673	15,14,04,71,169.85	2,01,961
30-Jul-2024	EQ	3,034.05	3,050.00	3,020.00	3,040.20	**3,023.00**	3,026.30	3,033.38	3,217.60	2,220.30	41,14,104	12,47,96,37,390.30	1,84,296
29-Jul-2024	EQ	3,023.90	3,055.00	3,023.55	3,018.05	**3,038.25**	3,040.20	3,038.43	3,217.60	2,220.30	37,69,275	11,45,26,61,155.40	1,70,155
26-Jul-2024	EQ	2,984.80	3,024.85	2,980.70	2,984.80	**3,018.60**	3,018.05	3,012.08	3,217.60	2,220.30	49,29,970	14,84,94,80,970.80	1,80,757
25-Jul-2024	EQ	2,962.00	3,000.95	2,954.15	2,991.40	**2,988.35**	2,984.80	2,980.72	3,217.60	2,220.30	62,59,938	18,65,91,22,151.40	2,21,753

Reliance Price Volume 7 Days Data

the market for some time to calm your mind, otherwise, in an attempt to recover the loss, such loss-making traders take bigger positions and make more losses.

It is also worth mentioning here that I do not encourage keeping stop losses in my methods. Keep a stop loss here and book a limited loss. This has been explained theoretically; but I have tried to make such scientific methods, by which profit can be earned without loss. Although, stop loss will also be used in some of the methods mentioned in the book, but it will be at a very limited level. You will be able to understand the description of many of my methods later in the book.

Whatever methods I am going to describe in the book, I have tried to explain in both the ways by giving practical examples –

1. What would have happened if you had traded by keeping a stop loss in this method?
2. What would have happened if you had not kept a stop loss in this method and had traded by averaging?

So in the coming chapters, I will explain it to you in more detail.

5. Keep booking profits in your profitable positions

In your childhood, you must have read in school that 'greed is a bad thing'. But most traders are very reluctant to follow this rule because they often find that in a bull market, after they book their profit, the stock rockets and then they regret that had they not booked the profit, they would have made 120 per cent profit today instead of 6 per cent.

I have used the term '6 per cent profit' here because in most of my methods, I have kept a standard profit target of 6 per cent; because as I have mentioned in the beginning of the book, if ₹ 20,000 is rotated with a profit target of 6 per cent, then ₹ 1 crores can be made in 108 trades.

This is the mistake traders make here. They forget that if they book a profit of 6 per cent and then invest the same money in the trade and book profit once again, then the two profits of 6 per cent each add up to a profit of 12 per cent.

The price of Kotak Mahindra Bank was ₹ 1,946.20 in May 2022 and at the time of writing the book, its price in August 2024 is ₹ 1,769.35. This means that if someone had held the shares of Kotak Mahindra Bank for two years, he would have lost about 9 per cent.

However, I booked profits of 6 per cent each four times in these two years by trading in Kotak Mahindra Bank. This means that I got a return of 24 per cent, because the original money came back to use.

In fact, the returns were more than 24 per cent—around 30 per cent—because firstly, I do not feed in the profit target. Whenever the stock shows a profit of more than 6 per cent, I book profit only then. So, in one trade, the profit was 6.43 per cent, in another, 6.82 per cent. Secondly, I also reinvest almost half of the profit by adding it back to the principal. So, the profit became even more, because after every trade, the principal increased a little.

I had also shown the balance sheet of profit booking of my consolidated breakout method on YouTube to my YouTube followers. They must have remembered it. Rest, new readers need not worry; I will explain this in detail later.

Now I will give you some basic information about what a candlestick chart is. Then in the next chapter, I will teach you to prepare a candlestick chart by hand without the help of any chart software.

The candlestick chart was invented by the Japanese after about 280 years of modification. In the markets of that time, Japanese traders used to earn the most profit. They used to make a structure that looked like a candle. From that, they used to guess the direction of the market.

The candle burns itself and gives light to others. In the same way, candlestick charts can also show you light on the path of the stock market.

In the next chapter, we will learn to prepare a candlestick chart by hand without any software.

❑

2

How to Create a Candlestick Chart by Hand without any Software?

You must have been surprised after reading the heading of this chapter that can candlestick charts be made by hand? Of course, they can be made. Even a child studying in the third grade can make them easily.

You must have seen the advertisement of charting softwares worth ₹ 50,000 to ₹ 1,00,000 in the stock market. People charge you lakhs of rupees for teaching candlestick chart reading. They sell you expensive software and claim to teach you trading!

However, in such training sessions, in most chart pattern books and chart pattern courses, you are shown the shapes of chart patterns described in technical analysis books and their names are told, which are Japanese names; like – I am writing some names here as examples –

1. Engulfing
2. Hammer
3. Doji
4. Hanging man
5. Shooting star
6. Harami
7. Marubozu

There are many such chart patterns and many names. If all of them are described and explained by showing their diagrams that if such a pattern is formed then the stock will fall and if such a pattern is formed then the stock will rise, then a book can be made on this. However, you do not get any benefit in practical trading from such books, such training sessions and such paid courses bought by paying a huge amount; because practical trading is an art. It is very difficult to do it by looking at the chart like this; like today, if a bearish Harami candle chart pattern is formed in a stock, then you will think that it will fall and you will do short selling in it. Then the next day, a bullish Marubozu candle will be formed in it and the person teaching you will wash his hands off the matter by saying, "Brother, keep a stop loss". Or they see the new pattern that has formed from bearish to bullish and start explaining that if you had booked your loss here and taken a new trade, you would have earned twice as much.

But let me tell you honestly that you can never earn profit in share trading by just memorising the names of such chart patterns and imbibing their pictures in your mind.

If someone wants to learn English and attends an English course, then most of the time, he is left after memorising the rules of English grammar and tenses; but he does not know English. Cannot an illiterate child of a native English-speaking country, who does not know tenses and grammar, speak English? You know that that child speaks better English than children of countries speaking other languages, without learning tenses and grammar.

So, it is all about practical knowledge. So if you have bought my book, do not expect me to show you screenshots of chart patterns software and teach you the clichéd names of patterns like Hanging man, Doji, Hammer, Harami etc. I will teach you my own invented methods of drawing candlestick charts by hand and using them in the practical market, so that you can become a truly profitable trader.

Let us start learning to make a candlestick chart by hand. For this, you need four data of any stock -

1. Open price
2. Close price
3. High price
4. Low price

For example, let us select the data of Nifty 50 of 9th August, 2024, to make a candle by hand. After the market closed on 9th August, 2024, the above four parameters of Nifty 50 were as follows -

1. Open price = 24,380.85
2. Close price = 24,367.50
3. High price = 24,419.75
4. Low price = 24,311.20

Now these four data have to be arranged in descending order. That is, they have to be arranged from top to bottom. In other words, the highest among them (naturally the high price will always be the highest) will come on top. That is, in a candlestick chart, the high price always comes at the top and the low price always comes at the bottom. Only the two prices in the middle, open-close or close-open, will come in a changed order according to the bullish or bearish candle.

This is very easy; even a third class student can do it easily. Let us write the above four data in descending order, then you will understand how the highest price is written at the top, then the one lower than that, then the one lower than that. The lowest price is written at the end and the candle will be ready.

1. High price = 24,419.75
2. Open price = 24,386.85
3. Close price = 24,367.50
4. Low Price = 24,311.20

To visualise this, let us draw it as a candle.

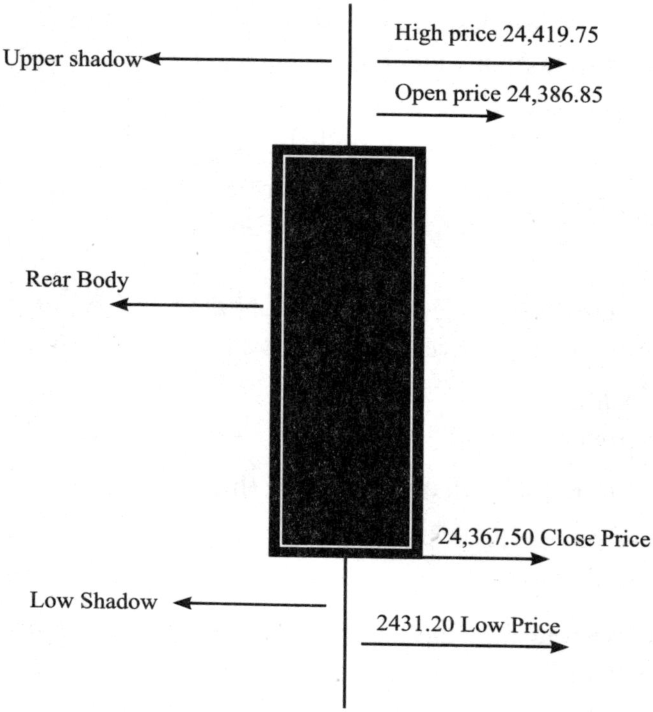

High price 24,419.75

Upper shadow

Open price 24,386.85

Rear Body

24,367.50 Close Price

Low Shadow

2431.20 Low Price

In this, high and low are shown as straight lines, which are called upper shadow and lower shadow respectively.

Open and close are shown in a square rear body, in which if the open is high, then it will go up and if the close is low, then it will go down.

In this way, the candle that is formed is called Bearish Candle, because in this, the open was near the high. This means that the market opened, then went up, and after that it fell and closed near the low price. That is why this Bearish candle is formed.

If you show it in red or black, then anyone can understand by looking at it that it is a bearish candle.

If you have this ability (which is usually found in a class 3 student too), then by looking at the price data, you can understand that "if the open price is high and the close price is low, then a bearish candle will be formed". That is, if the market closes at a level (close price) lower than the level at which it opens (open price), then the candle of that day is a bearish candle.

So there is no need for you to buy a charting software by paying ₹ 50,000 that tells you that a bearish candle has formed today by showing you a red-black candle. You will understand by looking at the data itself whether this candle is bearish or bullish.

Now let us understand an example of a bullish candle. The open-close, high-low for Tata Motors stock on 9th August, 2024 were as follows –

Open = 1,055.00

Close = 1,068.10

High = 1,082.95

Low = 1,052.05

Now, arranging it from top to bottom (high to low):

High = 1,082.95

Close = 1,068.10

Open = 1,055.00

Low = 1,052.05

This is how a bullish candle is formed.

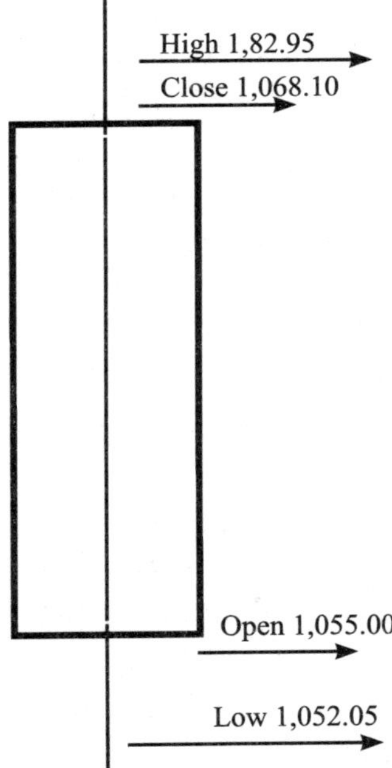

That is, when the close price is high and the open price is low, a bullish candle will be formed. The simple rule in a bullish candle is that the stock should close above the price at which it opened. Bullish candles are shown in green or white colour.

It can also be understood in this way that if the close price is near the high price, a bullish candle is formed and if the close price is near the low price, a bearish candle is formed.

I think you have learnt to prepare bullish and bearish candles by hand and identify them.

The upper shadow of any candle will always have the high price. Its lower shadow will always have the low price.

It is decided whether the candle is bullish or bearish only by looking at the rear body in the middle. A simple rule to remember is that if the candle is open upward (the open is near the high) then a bearish candle will be formed. In other words, the stock opened near the high and then gradually fell and closed near the low; hence, a bearish candle is formed.

On the contrary, if the open price is downward, then a bullish candle is formed. In other words, the stock opened near the low and closed near the high while rising, hence a bullish candle is formed.

I think, now you have learnt to make a candlestick chart by hand. Still, if someone is not able to understand, then they will definitely understand by reading the further chapters.

If you want, you can go to my YouTube channel, 'Mahesh Chandra Kaushik', and watch the video of class 6 (Technical Analysis) in the playlist named 'Mahesh Kaushik Ki Pathshala'. In it, I have explained to you how to make a candlestick chart manually on the board and have also explained the method of trading mentioned in the next chapter.

If you are already learning from me on YouTube, then the next chapter will help you a lot in understanding the practical examples of what you have learnt in the above video and you will understand how easy it is to trade by simply identifying the formation of bullish and bearish candles using my practical method, as compared to memorising the heavy names of chart patterns with Japanese names like Spinning Top, Dark Cloud Cover, Evening Star, Marubozu, Dragonfly, Three Black Crows, Three White Soldiers etc.!

❑

3

Practical Method of Making Profit based on Monthly Bullish Candle

As I have already told, I will not just show you the pictures of chart patterns and make you memorise the theoretical names that if such a chart is made, then this will happen, and if such a chart is made, then this will happen. I will tell you practical methods of how you can earn profit in the share market. After all, if you have bought this book, then your purpose is to learn to earn profit in the share market.

To see the names of chart patterns and their pictures, you can access Google, type 'Free Technical Analysis PDF' and download many PDFs and read such books for free. However, as many of you already know, it is very difficult to earn money in the share market by just seeing the names and pictures of chart patterns, unless you learn to use them in practice. So, in this chapter, I will tell you a simple and practical way to identify whether the monthly candle is bullish or bearish and take the trade.

As I taught you in the previous chapter, four main data points are required to create a candlestick chart -

Open Price (the price of the stock when the market opens)

Close Price (the price of the stock when the market closes)

High Price (Highest price of the day)

Low Price (Lowest price of the day)

First of all, arrange these four data points in descending order.

The highest price comes at the top (High Price) and the lowest price comes at the bottom (Low Price).

In between are the open and close prices, which decide whether the candle is bullish (going up) or bearish (going down).

Bullish candle — When the close price is higher than the open price, meaning, the stock closes at a higher price at the end of the day.

Bearish candle — When the close price is lower than the open price, meaning the stock closes at a lower price at the end of the day.

First of all, remember that when we try to bind buying and selling in the stock market to a single rule, then it is an impossible task, because the prices of shares always keep going up and down in a zig -zag manner. So you should not think that you will get profit every time by a single method; but if you keep faith in that method and keep working on the same pattern, then you remain in overall profit. What I mean to say here is that no method has a 100 per cent success rate; but if your method has a success rate of 70 to 90 per cent, then you can get overall profit in it. The method which I will teach you now, I will show its practical back test with historical data in Reliance, TCS, and HDFC Bank, the three companies with the highest market cap, so that you will understand how you can remain a consistently profitable trader with just this one method.

This method can also be used in two ways -

1. **With Stop Loss:** My old readers and followers know that I never like to keep a stop loss and I do not suggest keeping a stop loss in most of my methods. But if you do not keep a stop loss, then you should not use these methods in future options and margin trading etc. In intraday trading, this method should not be used as it is based on monthly candles. Therefore, I will do a back test of this method on historical data and in that, I will show you the results of both the methods—what would have happened if you had used it with stop loss and what would have been the results if you had used it without stop loss?

2. **Without Stop Loss:** I myself always prefer to use these methods without stop loss. Actually, there are three types of people who trade in the market -

   1. Traders who create future option positions much larger than their capital.
   2. Traders who create margin trading positions a little more than their capital.
   3. Traders who take delivery positions in the cash market according to their capacity.

Therefore, I fall in the third category out of the above three categories, because it helps in getting good sleep at night with balanced blood pressure and sugar levels. We remain stress free since the shares are bought after paying the full amount, we can easily hold them. Also, our boat never goes forward and backward. The boat may be moving slowly in this, but by always moving forward, it reaches the destination faster than those whose boats sometimes go ahead and sometimes behind. You must have read the story of the tortoise and the rabbit in your childhood. In this, like the tortoise, we move ahead slowly, while booking profits.

In this method, by not keeping a stop loss, by being a little patient, and by averaging smartly, we can exit without loss. Therefore, I will explain both the methods to you. Whatever category of trader you are, use it accordingly.

If you fall in the first and second category then you are compelled to keep a stop loss, otherwise you may incur a huge loss if the trade goes against your will.

If you trade within limits and according to your ability like me, then instead of keeping a stop loss, you can use my method without stop loss.

Now let us start understanding this method without any delay.

1. First of all, look at the monthly candle of the stock. Monthly candle does not mean calendar month but the future option month. In Indian stock markets, future options expire on the last Thursday of every month. So, the month I have taken here starts from the Friday after the expiry on the last Thursday of the month and continues till

the last Thursday of the next month. For example, after the expiry of March on 31st March, 2023 a new series started which expired on 27th April, 2023. Hence, here month means from 31st March, 2023 to 27th April, 2023.

In the same way, you can see in the table below how the remaining months of the year 2023-24 are considered on the basis of expiry. This will give you a clear idea of how the month is taken on the basis of expiry in my methods, because most of the volume is based on future options. So, I select the month on the basis of expiry.

Future Expiry Month Options
31stMarch, 2023 to 27thApril, 2023
28thApril, 2023 to 25thMay, 2023
26thMay, 2023 to 29thJune, 2023
30thJune, 2023 to 27thJuly, 2023
28thJuly, 2023 to 31st August, 2023
1st September, 2023 to 28th September, 2023
29th September 2023 to 26th October 2023
27th October, 2023 to 30th November, 2023
1st December, 2023 to 28th December, 2023
29th December, 2023 to 25th January, 2024
26th January, 2024 to 29th February, 2024
1st March, 2024 to 28th March, 2024
29th March, 2024 to 25th April, 2024

2. Look at the following four price s in a monthly candle—open, close, high, low?

   As per the method mentioned in the previous chapter about making a candle manually, decide whether the candle formed this month is a bullish candle or a bearish candle.

3. If the close price (the close price of the last day of the month is considered as the close price for the entire month) is higher than the open price (the open price of the day when a new series starts in the month), then the candle of that month is a bullish candle.

4. If the close price is lower than the open price, then the candle of that month is a bearish candle.
5. Now you can trade in this in two ways.
   (a) If you are trading in future options, then you have to buy in the month when a bullish candle is formed and you have to short sell in the month when a bearish candle is formed.
   (b) If you are trading on the basis of delivery in the cash segment, you will buy only on bullish candles and use the formation of bearish candles as stop loss.

   In this chapter, I will explain you by back testing only on cash segment data; but traders who wish to use these methods in futures or in buying call puts in the option market can do so as per the rules given for the cash segment.
6. If the close price of the month for which you are making the candle is higher than the open price of the month, then a bullish candle will be formed.

   For example, in the month of expiry from 31st March, 2023 to 27th April, 2023, the open price of Reliance share was 2,255, high price 2,424.95, lowest price 2,254.70, and close price 2,377.05. Therefore, its candle will be formed like this:

So, this is a bullish candle. On the day of the start of the new series of that month, i.e., on 28th April, 2023, you had to create a position by buying Reliance shares in the cash market as soon as the market opened. (Traders with future options can take a position in future or buy calls; but often taking a position in F&O is an out of the pocket approach and since stop loss is mandatory in it, I prefer to do it in cash. I also suggest that if you have a lot of capital and want to take a big position, then at least take it in margin instead of futures option, where you can decide the lot size yourself and take a position according to your capacity.)

Now, since a bullish candle (i.e. the monthly candle of the previous series was bullish) has formed, everyone would want to take a position in the new series; so due to the high crowd, i.e., high demand, the stock opens higher on that day and you have to take an expensive position.

So, my simple method is that you buy and hold the stock in the last half hour on the expiry day of the series.

Now you will ask that without knowing the close price of the expiry day how will we know whether the candle of that month is going to be bullish or bearish? So my dear readers! You can make a candle by considering whatever price is prevailing in the last half hour of the expiry day as the close price. The close price is also the average of the price of the last half hour, hence whatever fluctuation is to happen on the expiry day has already happened in the whole day and there is usually no possibility of any big move in the last half hour. Well, if you want, you can also buy in the last half hour of the expiry day or if you do not like to do so, then you can easily buy it a little expensive on the first day of the new series after the candle is formed.

In this book, I am showing you this method by doing a practical back test on the data of Reliance Industries, which I am doing assuming that you bought in the last half hour of the expiry day. Hence, in this back test, I am using the Last Trading Price (LTP) as the buy price.

7. After buying, the profit target for the next month should be around 3 per cent. Now you will ask why only 3 per cent? Why not 1-2-4-5-6? So, actually in technical analysis, we are buying for trading and after my 20 years of experience in the stock market and my long research, I feel that the principles of physics apply to the stock market and the probability of profit of the value of $\pi = 22/7$, i.e., 3.14, is the highest for short term trade and in my methods of swing trading, I consider the probability of profit is equal to two π, i.e., around 6.28 per cent, to be the best. So here we have to take a profit target of around 3 per cent. I am including a separate chapter named 'Physics of Share Market' in this book on what 'π' is for those who are not students of science.
8. If you are buying in the cash market, then you do not have to keep any stop loss; but in such a case, you have to keep in mind that you should use this method only in blue chip stocks, so that there is no possibility of the stock falling too much or being delisted etc. Instead of keeping a stop loss in this, the next time when a bullish candle is formed, then the averaging will appear automatically by buying again. If you are not able to understand this fact here, then do not panic. You will understand everything when I will explain it further with the help of practical data.
9. If you are trading in future options or margin the low of the candle on the basis of which you have made the purchase, that is, the lowest level of that month, will be your stop loss and profit is not booked in the whole month. If a bearish candle is formed in the next month, then that will be considered as your stop loss, that is, the lowest level of the previous month or the formation of the monthly bearish candle—whichever happens first—that will be the stop loss. If you are not able to understand, then do not panic. I have yet to explain it with an example.

In short, the point is that if the monthly candle is bullish, then buy it, and try to take a target of 3 per cent in the next month and if the target is not achieved, plus the next month's candle is bearish, then either keep calm, hold or consider the stop loss trigger. If the lowest level of the previous month is reached in the middle of the month, then consider the stop loss there. If two consecutive candles are bullish and the target is not achieved, then do not buy again, and hold the previous position only. After understanding all these theoretical points, now in the next chapter, I will do a practical back test on the historical data of Reliance, HDFC Bank and TCS, the three companies with the highest market cap in the Indian stock markets at present, and will inform you about the result.

You can also understand this topic in a more visual way by visiting my YouTube channel and watching the video of 'Mahesh Kaushik Ki Pathshaala Class 6 Technical Analysis'.

❑

4

Back Test of Monthly Candle-based Trading on Top 3 Large Cap Companies

Based on the rules explained in the previous chapter, let us now do a back test on 16 months of data of 3 large cap companies and see what the results are. For this, you have to download their historical data from NSE and do both types of back tests by averaging with and without stop loss along with me. You can see the 16 months back test of swing trading on the basis of monthly candles in Reliance stock with stop loss in the following tables –

Month	Open	High	Low	Close	Candle
31st March 2023 to 27th April 2023	2255.00	2424.95	2254.70	2377.05	Bullish
28th April, 2023 to 25th May, 2023	2,382.00	2509.50	2381.75	2439.95	Bullish
May 26th , 2023 to June 29th , 2023	2,458.00	2,584.00	2,450.75	2,529.50	Bullish
June 30th , 2023 to July 27th , 2023	2,546.40	2,856.00	2,469.30	2,502.70	Bearish
July 28th , 2023 to August 31st , 2023	2,512.05	2,582.80	2,399.90	2,407.00	Bearish
1st September, 2023 to 28th September, 2023	2,406.65	2,483.00	2,325.00	2,334.10	Bearish
29th September, 2023 to 26th October, 2023	2,341.08	2,369.10	2,220.30	2,226.50	Bearish
27th October, 2023 to 30th November, 2023	2,240.00	2,411.95	2,235.95	2,377.45	Bullish

1st December 2023 to 28th December 2023	2,378.00	2,612.00	2,377.60	2,605.55	Bullish
29th December 2023 to 25th January 2024	2,611.10	2,792.90	2,568.95	2,706.15	Bullish
26th January, 2024 to 29th February, 2024	2,729.00	2,999.90	2,720.35	2,921.60	Bullish
1st March, 2024 to 28th March, 2024	2,927.00	3,024.90	2,825.80	2,971.70	Bullish
29th March, 2024 to 25th April, 2024	2,984.95	2,988.00	2,883.00	2,919.95	Bearish
26th April, 2024 to 30th May, 2024	2,927.90	2,984.45	2,768.00	2,849.70	Bearish
31st May, 2024 to 27th June, 2024	2,862.60	3,075.00	2,718.60	3,061.10	Bullish
28th June, 2024 to 25th July, 2024	3,062.05	3,217.60	2,926.00	2,984.80	Bearish

Now, if you had bought on the monthly bullish candle formed as per the above table and kept the stop loss at the lowest level of the previous month, and if the stop loss is not hit first, then considering the formation of a bearish candle as the stop loss, if you had bought and sold 100 shares of Reliance, then the result would have been as per the following table—

Month	Buy Price	Target	Stop Loss	Target Date	Stop Loss Date	Profit	Loss
31st March, 2023 to 27th April, 2023	2382.00	2453.45	2254.70	9th May, 2023	Nil	7145	0
28th April, 2023 to 25th May, 2023	2445.00	2518.35	2381.75	13th June, 2023	Nil	7335	0
26th May , 2023 to 29th June , 2023	2531.00	2606.95	2450.75	3rd July, 2023	Nil	7595	0
30th June , 2023 to 27th July, 2023	0.00	0.00	0.00	Nil	Nil	0	0
From 28th July, 2023 31st August, 2023	0.00	0.00	0.00	Nil	Nil	0	0

1st September, 2023 to 28th September, 2023	0.00	0.00	0.00	Nil	Nil	0	0
29th September, 2023 to 26th October, 2023	0.00	0.00	0.00	Nil	Nil	0	0
From 27th October 2023 to 30th November 2023	2,380.00	2451.40	2235.95	19th December 2023	Nil	7140	0
From 1st December, 2023 to 28th December, 2023	2606.00	2684.20	2377.60	11th January, 2023	Nil	7820	0
29th December, 2023 to 25th January, 2024	2712.00	2793.35	2568.95	29th January, 2024	Nil	8135	0
26th January, 2024 to 29th February, 2024	2931.00	3018.95	2720.35	4th March, 2024	Nil	8795	0
1st March 2024 to 28th March 2024	2971	3060.15	2825.80	Nil	Nil	0	0
March 29th , 2024 to April 25th , 2024	0	0	0	Nil	Nil	0	5400
April 26th , 2024 to May 30th , 2024	0	0	0	Nil	Nil	0	
May 31st , 2024 to June 27th , 2024	3058.00	3149.75	2718.60	5th July, 2024	Nil	9175	
June 28th , 2024 to July 25th , 2024	0	0	0	Nil	Nil		
					TOTAL	63140	5400
				Net Profit	57740		

For many readers who do not know much about mathematics, I have presented the details of the trading described in the above two tables in a month-wise descriptive form. If you read this description as well as see the above two tables, you will understand the whole thing. I will explain only Reliance shares by doing a descriptive back test in this way. After that you will learn well what has been explained in this type of table. Therefore, in the next two shares, TCS and HDFC Bank, I will not give you such a complete description, but will be able to explain easily by just showing the data in the table. Therefore, read the monthly description given below along with the above tables, so that you understand well.

First Month

This back test has been taken for the future option expiry month from 31st March, 2023 to 27th April, 2023. The data of open, high, low and close for this month was as follows –

Open Price = 2,255.00

High Price = 2,424.95

Low Price = 2,254.70

Close Price = 2,377.05

Based on the above data, you can see that this month's candle is a bullish one. Therefore, to explain to you in the example at what price you bought it, I have, to be completely honest, assumed that you bought it at the last trading price of that day, i.e. LTP, above the close price.

Here, if you had bought 100 shares of Reliance in the last half hour of the expiry day, considering the current price as the close price and making a candle by hand, then your purchase price (I have considered the last trading price of the last day of the said expiry month as your purchase price) would have been ₹ 2,382.00 per share.

Now, as I have told you in the previous chapter that for trading, the probability of getting a profit target equal to the value of π, i.e., 3.14 per cent, or approximately 3 percent is the highest, so if you had taken a target of 3 per cent above this purchase price, then your profit target would have been 3 per cent above your purchase price of 2,382.00, i.e., ₹ 2,453.45.

From the historical data of Reliance for the next trading month, you can see that on 9th May, 2023, you would have achieved this target and on buying 100 shares, you would have made a profit of 2,453.45-2,382.00 = 71.45×100 = 7,145 rupees. Here, for convenience of calculation, I have not included brokerage and other charges in the calculation.

Here in the above data, the low price of 2,254.70 in the month of purchase was the stop loss and from the historical data of Reliance on NSE, you can see that the stop loss of 2,254.70 was not hit anywhere in the entire month.

Second Month

This back test has been taken for the future option expiry month from 28th April, 2023 to 25th May, 2023. The Open-High-Low and

Close data for this month were as follows—

Open Price = 2,382.00

High Price = 2,509.50

Low Price = 2,381.75

Close Price = 2,439.95

Based on the above data, you can see that this month's candle has been a bullish candle. Hence, to explain to you in the example at what price you bought it, I have honestly assumed that you bought it at the last trading price of that day, i.e., LTP, which is above the close price.

Here, if you had bought 100 shares of Reliance on the expiry day by making a candle by hand, considering whatever price was prevailing in the last half hour as the close price, then your purchase price (I have considered the last trading price of the last day of the said expiry month as your purchase price) would have been ₹ 2,445.00 per share.

Now, as I told you in the previous chapter, the most likely way to trade is to get a profit target equal to the value of π, i.e. 3.14 per cent or approximately 3 per cent. So, if you had taken a target of 3 per cent above this purchase price, your profit target would have been 3 per cent above your purchase price of 2,445.00, i.e. rupees 2,518.35.

From the historical data of Reliance for the next trading month, you can see that on 13th June, 2023, you would have achieved this target and would have made a profit of 2,518.35-2,445.00 = 73.35×100 = 7,335 rupees on the purchase of 100 shares. Here, for convenience of calculation, I have not included brokerage and other charges in the calculation.

Here in the above data, the low price of the purchase month was 2,381.75, which was the stop loss. From the historical data of Reliance on NSE, you can see that the stop loss of 2,381.75 was not hit anywhere in the entire month.

Third Month

This back test has been taken for the future option expiry month from 26th May, 2023 to 29th June, 2023. The data of open, high, low and close for this month were as follows-

Open Price = 2,458.00

High Price = 2,584.00

Low Price = 2,450.75

Close Price = 2,529.50

Based on the above data, you can see that this month's candle has been a bullish candle. Hence, to explain to you in the example at what price you bought the stock, I have honestly assumed that you bought it at the last trading price of that day, i.e., LTP, which is above the close price.

Here, if you had bought 100 shares of Reliance on the expiry day by making a candle by hand, considering whatever price was prevailing in the last half hour as the close price, then your purchase price (I have considered the last trading price of the last day of the said expiry month as your purchase price) would have been ₹ 2,531.00 per share.

Now, as I told you in the previous chapter, the most likely way to trade is to get a profit target equal to the value of π, i.e., 3.14 per cent, or approximately 3 per cent. So, if you had taken a target of 3 per cent above this purchase price, your profit target would have been 3 per cent above your purchase price of 2,531.00, i.e., 2,606.95.

From the historical data of Reliance for the next trading month, you can see that on 3rd July, 2023, you would have achieved this target and you would have made a profit of 2,606.95-2,531.00 = 75.95×100 = 7,595 rupees on buying 100 shares. Here, for convenience, I have not included brokerage and other charges in the calculation.

Here in the above data, the low price of the purchase month was 2,450.75, which was the stop loss. From the historical data of Reliance on NSE, you can see that the stop loss of 2,450.75 was not hit anywhere in the entire month.

Fourth Month

This back test has been taken for the future option expiry month from 30th June, 2023 to July 27, 2023. The data of open, high, low and close for this month were as follows –

Open Price = 2,546.40

High Price = 2,856.00

Low Price = 2,469.30

Close Price = 2,502.70

Based on the above data, you can see that the candle of this month has formed a bearish candle. According to the rule of this method, no purchase has to be made in the month in which a bearish candle is formed.

For those who keep stop loss, if profit is not booked in the position taken in the previous month and the stop loss is also not triggered, then the formation of a bearish candle indicates a second stop loss and the stop loss is considered triggered as soon as such a candle is formed. Here, since there is no previous position held, neither anything is bought nor sold this month.

Fifth Month

This back test has been taken for the future option expiry month from 28th July, 2023 to 31st August, 2023. The data of open, high, low and close for this month were as follows –

Open price = 2,512.05

High price = 2,582.80

Low price = 2,399.90

Close price = 2,407.00

Based on the above data, you can see that this month's candle has formed a bearish candle. According to the rule of this method, no purchase has to be made in the month in which a bearish candle is formed.

For those who keep a stop loss, if the profit is not booked in the position taken in the previous month and the stop loss is also not triggered, then the formation of a bearish candle indicates a second stop loss and the stop loss is considered triggered as soon as such a candle is formed. Here, since there is no previous position held, nothing is bought or sold this month.

Sixth Month

This back test has been taken for the future option expiry month from 1st September, 2023 to 28th September, 2023. The data of open, high, low and close for this month were as follows –

Open price = 2,406.65

High price = 2,483.00

Low price = 2,325.00

Close price = 2,334.10

Based on the above data, you can see that this month's candle has formed a bearish candle. According to the rule of this method, no purchase is to be made in the month in which a bearish candle is formed.

For those who keep a stop loss, if profit has not been booked in the position taken in the previous month and the stop loss has also not been triggered, then the formation of a bearish candle indicates a second stop loss and the stop loss is considered triggered as soon as such a candle is formed. Here, since there is no previous position held, nothing was bought or sold this month.

Seventh Month

This back test was conducted for the futures option expiry month from 29th September, 2023 to 26th October, 2023. The open, high, low and close data for this month were as follows—

Open Price = 2,341.08

High Price = 2,369.10

Low Price = 2,220.30

Close Price = 2,226.50

Based on the above data, you can see that this month's candle is a bearish candle. According to the rule of this method, no purchase is to be made in the month in which a bearish candle is formed.

For those who keep a stop loss, if profit has not been booked in the position taken in the previous month and the stop loss has also not been triggered, then the formation of a bearish candle indicates a second stop loss and the stop loss is considered triggered as soon as such a candle is formed. Here, since there is no previous position held, nothing is bought or sold this month.

Eighth Month

This back test was conducted for the futures option expiry month from 27th October, 2023 to 30th November, 2023. The open, high, low and close data for this month were as follows –

Open Price = 2,240.00

High Price = 2,411.95

Low Price = 2,235.95

Close Price = 2,377.45

Based on the above data, you can see that this month's candle has formed a bullish candle. Hence, to explain to you in the example at what price you bought the stock, I have, to be completely honest, assumed that you bought it at the last trading price of that day, i.e., the LTP, above the close price.

Here, if you had bought 100 shares of Reliance on the expiry day, by making a candle by hand, considering the current price in the last half hour as the close price, then your purchase price (I have considered the last trading price of the last day of the said expiry month as your purchase price) would have been ₹ 2,380.00 per share.

Now, as I told you in the previous chapter, for trading, to get a profit target equal to the value of π, i.e., 3.14 per cent, or approximately 3 per cent is most likely. So, if you had taken a target of 3 per cent above this purchase price, your profit target would have been 3per cent above your purchase price of 2,380.00, i.e. rupees 2,451.40.

From the historical data of Reliance for the next trading month, you can see that on 19th December, 2023, you would have achieved this target and you would have made a profit of 2,451.4-2,380.00 = 71.40×100 = 7,140 rupees on the purchase of 100 shares. Here, for convenience of calculation, I have not included brokerage and other charges in the calculation.

Here in the above data, the low price of 2,235.95 of the purchase month was the stop loss. From the historical data of Reliance on NSE, you can see that the stop loss of 2,235.95 was not hit anywhere in the entire month.

Ninth Month

This back test has been taken for the futures option expiry month from 1st December, 2023 to 28th December, 2023. The data of open, high, low and close of this month were as follows –

Open Price = 2,378.00

High Price = 2,612.00

Low Price = 2,377.60

Close Price = 2,605.55

Based on the above data, you can see that the candle of this month has formed a bullish candle. So, to explain to you in this example, at what price you bought the stock, I have honestly assumed that you bought it at the last trading price of that day, i.e. the LTP, which is above the close price.

Here, if you had bought 100 shares of Reliance in the last half hour of the expiry day, considering whatever price was prevailing as the close price and making a candle by hand, then your purchase price (I have considered the last trading price of the last day of the said expiry month as your purchase price) would have been ₹ 2,606.00 per share.

Now, as I have told you in the previous chapter, for trading, the probability of getting a profit target equal to the value of π, i.e. 3.14 per cent, or approximately 3 per cent is the highest, so if you had taken a target of 3 per cent above this purchase price, then your profit target would have been 3 per cent above your purchase price of 2,606.00, i.e. rupees 2,684.2.

From the historical data of Reliance for the next trading month, you can see that on 11th January, 2023, you would have achieved this target and on buying 100 shares, you would have made a profit of ₹ 2,684.2-2,606.00 = 78.20×100 = 7,820. Here, for convenience of calculation, I have not included brokerage and other charges in the calculation.

Here in the above data, the low price of 2,377.60 in the month of purchase was the stop loss. From the historical data of Reliance on NSE, you can see that the stop loss of 2,377.60 was not hit anywhere in the entire month.

Tenth Month

This back test has been taken for the futures option expiry month from 29th December, 2023 to 25th January, 2024. The open, high, low and close data for this month were as follows—

Open Price = 2,611.10

High Price = 2,792.90

Low Price = 2,568.95

Close Price = 2,706.15

Based on the above data, you can see that this month's candle has been a bullish candle. Hence, to explain to you in the example at what price you bought it, I have honestly assumed that you bought it at the last trading price of that day, i.e., LTP, which is above the close price.

Here, if you had bought 100 shares of Reliance on the expiry day by making a candle by hand, considering whatever price was prevailing in the last half hour as the close price, then your purchase price (I have considered the last trading price of the last day of the said expiry month as your purchase price) would have been ₹ 2,712.00 per share.

Now, as I told you in the previous chapter, for trading, the probability of getting a profit target equal to the value of π, i.e., 3.14 per cent, or approximately 3 per cent is the highest. So, if you had taken a target of 3 per cent above this purchase price, your profit target would have been 3 per cent above your purchase price of 2,712.00, i.e., ₹ 2,793.35.

From the historical data of Reliance for the next trading month, you can see that on 29th January, 2024, you would have achieved this target and you would have made a profit of 2,793.35-2,712.00 = 81.35×100= ₹ 8,135 on the purchase of 100 shares. Here, for convenience of calculation, I have not included brokerage and other charges in the calculation.

Here in the above data, the low price of the purchase month was 2,568.95, which was the stop loss. From the historical data of Reliance on NSE, you can see that the stop loss of 2,568.95 was not hit anywhere in the entire month.

Eleventh Month

This back test has been taken for the futures option expiry month from 26th January, 2024 to 29th February, 2024. The data of open, high, low and close for this month were as follows-

Open Price = 2,729.00

High Price = 2,999.9

Low Price = 2,720.35

Close Price = 2,921.60

Based on the above data, you can see that this month's candle has been a bullish candle. Hence, to explain to you in the example at what price you bought it, I have honestly assumed that you bought it at the last trading price of that day, i.e., LTP, which is above the close price.

Here, if you had bought 100 shares of Reliance in the last half hour of the expiry day, considering whatever price was prevailing as the close price and making a candle by hand, then your purchase price (I have considered the last trading price of the last day of the said expiry month as your purchase price) would have been ₹ 2,931.00 per share.

Now, as I told you in the previous chapter, for trading, the probability of getting a profit target equal to the value of π, i.e. 3.14 per cent, or approximately 3 per cent is the highest. So, if you had taken a target of 3 per cent above this purchase price, your profit target would have been 3 per cent above your purchase price of 2,931.00, i.e. 3,018.95.

From the historical data of Reliance for the next trading month, you can see that on 4th March, 2024, you would have achieved this target and you would have made a profit of 3,018.95-2,931.00 = 87.95×100 = 8,795 rupees on buying 100 shares. Here, for convenience of calculation, I have not included brokerage and other charges in the calculation.

Here in the above data, the low price of the purchase month was 2,720.35, which was the stop loss. From the historical data of Reliance on NSE, you can see that the stop loss of 2,720.35 was not hit anywhere in the entire month.

Twelfth Month

This back test has been taken for the futures option expiry month from 1st March, 2024 to 28th March, 2024. The data of open, high, low and close for this month were as follows-

Open Price = 2,927.00

High Price = 3,024.90

Low Price = 2,825.80

Close Price = 2,971.70

Based on the above data, you can see that this month's candle has been a bullish candle. Hence, to explain to you in the example at what price you bought the stock, I have honestly assumed that you bought it at the last trading price of that day, i.e. LTP, which is above the close price.

Here, if you had bought 100 shares of Reliance on the expiry day by making a candle by hand, considering whatever price was prevailing in the last half hour of the expiry day as the close price, then your purchase price (I have considered the last trading price of the last day of the said expiry month as your purchase price) would have been ₹ 2,791.00 per share.

Now, as I told you in the previous chapter, for trading, the probability of getting a profit target equal to the value of π, i.e., 3.14 per cent, or approximately 3per cent is the highest. So, if you had taken a target of 3per cent above this buy price, your profit target would have been 3per cent above your buy price of 2,791.00, i.e. 3,060.15.

From the historical data of Reliance for the next trading month, you can see that this target was not hit in the entire month.

Here, in the above data, the low price of the buy month was 2,825.80, which was the stop loss. From the historical data of Reliance on NSE, you can see that the stop loss of 2,825.80 was not hit anywhere in the entire month.

In other words, in the back test of Reliance, there has been only one occasion in the entire year, when your profit was not booked during the month and the primary stop loss, which was the minimum level of the previous month, was also not hit; but if you wanted to trade with stop loss by considering the next month's candle, which was a bearish candle, as a secondary stop loss, then you should have booked a loss. I will explain this fact in the details of the next month.

Thirteenth Month

This back test has been taken for the futures option expiry months from 29th March, 2024 to 25th April, 2024. The data of open, high, low and close for this month were as follows –

Open Price = 2,984.95

High Price = 2,988.00

Low Price = 2,883.00

Close Price = 2,919.95

Based on the above data, you can see that this month's candle has formed a bearish candle. According to the rule of this method, no purchase has to be made in the month in which a bearish candle is formed.

For those who keep a stop loss, if profit has not been booked in the position taken in the previous month and the stop loss has also not been triggered, then the formation of a bearish candle indicates the second stop loss. As soon as such a candle is formed, the stop loss is considered triggered. Hence, if loss was booked on LTP due to the formation of a bearish candle here, then a loss of ₹ 5,400 would have occurred. Now, after making profit for 11 months, if a loss of ₹ 5,400 was booked in 1 month, then overall you would have been in profit and if the fall was longer after booking the loss, then you would have been saved from that fall. Another advantage of booking a loss is that we get back our remaining capital, which is used for trading in future.

But those who do not keep a stop loss should always keep in mind that they should invest by dividing their capital into 10 parts per share. Investment without stop loss should be done only in the cash market. If you do not keep a stop loss, then do not use margin trading or future market. In other words, in the method without stop loss, we should invest less capital at one time, because in this, whenever a bullish candle is formed, we have to buy back for average and then keep a target of 3 per cent of the average price.

Here, if you did not place a stop loss and did not book the said loss of ₹ 5,400, then on 27th June 2024, you would have achieved your target of ₹ 3,060.15 and there would have been no need to average anywhere, because before this target, a bearish candle was always formed. However, here, 27th June 2024 was the expiry day. On the day this target was formed, if you booked profit in the previous holding, then you could not buy back on the same day due to the formation of a bullish candle for the next month, because the system of some brokers starts considering selling first and buying back in the same day as intraday. However, nowadays, this has been corrected in the system of most brokers. If you still had such a problem, then you could have made a new purchase on the first day of the next series.

Fourteenth Month

This back test has been taken for the futures option expiry month from 26th April, 2024 to 30th May, 2024. The data of open, high, low and close for this month were as follows –

Open Price = 2,927.90

High Price = 2,984.45

Low Price = 2,768.00

Close Price = 2,849.7

Based on the above data, you can see that the candle of this month has formed a bearish candle. According to the rule of this method, no purchase has to be made in the month in which a bearish candle is formed.

Fifteenth Month

This back test has been taken for the futures option expiry month from 31st May, 2024 to 27th June, 2024. The data of open, high, low and close for this month was as follows –

Open Price = 2,862.60

High Price = 3,075.00

Low Price = 2,718.60

Close Price = 3,061.10

Based on the above data, you can see that this month's candle has formed a bullish candle. Hence, to explain to you in the example at what price you bought, I have, to be completely honest, assumed that you bought it at the last trading price of that day, i.e., LTP, which was above the close price.

Here, if you had bought 100 shares of Reliance in the last half hour of the expiry day, considering the current price as the close price and making a candle by hand, then your purchase price (I have considered the last trading price of the last day of the said expiry month as your purchase price) would have been ₹ 3,058.00 per share.

If you were trading in the cash market with less capital and without a stop loss, then the target of the purchase you made in the twelfth month was ₹ 3,060.15 and you had kept that position on hold because you did not keep a stop loss. Its target would have also come on the expiry day. Now, how is it wise to book profit in the previous position at ₹ 3,060.15 and buy again at ₹ 3,058? Therefore, learning trading is like learning to swim in water. It is an art. You should also use your mind in this.

If the target of 3,060.15 had come somewhere in the middle of the whole month and we had sold, then we could have bought back on the expiry day on the basis of the formation of a bullish candle; but here the target is coming on the expiry day itself and we have already guessed that whatever is the last trading price today, this month's candle is going to be bullish, because the open price of the month was 2,862.60 and on the expiry day, the price is running above ₹ 3,000. So, it is natural that this month's candle is going to be bullish.

What I mean to say here is that if you had a previous position on hold, you could have held it for the next months instead of booking profit in it.

Now, as I have told you in the previous chapter that for trading, the probability of getting a profit target equal to the value of π, i.e., 3.14 per cent, or approximately 3 per cent is the highest. So, if you were making a new purchase, you could have kept a target of 3 per cent above this purchase price. So your profit target would have been 3 per cent above your purchase price of 3,058.00, i.e. rupees 3,149.75. And even if the previous position was on hold, we could have increased the target for it from 3,060.15 to 3,149.75 and held it for the next month.

From the historical data of Reliance for the next trading month, you can see that on 5th July, 2024, you would have achieved this target and on buying 100 shares, you would have made a profit of 3,149.75-3,058.00 = 91.75×100 = 9,175 rupees. Here, for convenience of calculation, I have not included brokerage and other charges in the calculation.

If you had booked profit now in the twelfth month position, you would have made a profit of 3,149.75-2,971 = 178.75×100 = 17,875 rupees. Here also, for convenience of calculation, I have not included brokerage and other charges in the calculation.

Here in the above data, the low price of 2,718.60 of the purchase month was the stop loss. From the historical data of Reliance on NSE, you can see that the stop loss of 2,718.60 was not hit anywhere in the entire month.

Sixteenth Month

This back test has been taken for the futures option expiry month from 28th June, 2024 to 25th July, 2024. The data of open, high, low and close for this month were as follows-

Open Price = 3,062.05

High Price = 3,217.60

Low Price = 2,926.00

Close Price = 2,984.80

Based on the above data, you can see that this month's candle is a bearish candle. According to the rule of this method, no purchase is to be made in the month in which a bearish candle is formed.

For those who keep a stop loss, if profit has not been booked in the position taken in the previous month and the stop loss has also not been triggered, then the formation of a bearish candle indicates the second stop loss and the stop loss is considered triggered as soon as such a candle is formed. Here, since there is no previous position held, therefore, nothing was bought or sold this month.

Summary—You read and understood the back test of 16 months of Reliance. Overall, if you had traded on margin or futures with a stop loss, the stop loss would have been triggered only once and after deducting the loss, you would have made an overall profit of ₹ 57,740.

If you had traded in cash with less capital, you would not have had to book a loss of ₹ 5,400 and you would have got further profit on the hold position, so you would have made a profit of ₹ 71,840.

Now, if you have read the above description carefully, then you have learned how to do this back test. To avoid the book becoming too big, I have explained to you the 16-month back test of the second largest market cap company, TCS, in Reliance above. Without giving the full details, I will explain directly on the basis of the table.

Based on 16 months of TCS data, you can see how the candle was formed in this table—

Now, as explained in the Reliance example in this chapter, if you had taken the trade by keeping a stop loss, then in these 16 months, you would have booked a profit of ₹ 81,040 and a loss of ₹ 15,885 without including brokerage and charges. Overall, you would have made a net profit of ₹ 65,155.

Now, what would have happened if instead of booking a loss, you had held the position? These are such lines on which many readers will raise questions. They will say that what if one did not keep a stop loss and the company got delisted? Some readers will say that what if one did not keep a stop loss and the stock kept falling in the bear market?

Now, I have explained both types of methods. Those who are of trader mind-set and are trading future options or on margin should keep a stop loss. Those who are investing only in the top 10 market cap large companies with less than their own capital and whenever a bullish candle is formed, if the previous position is held but profit is not booked

TCS 16-Month Data and Corresponding Candles

Month	Open	High	Low	Close	LTP	Candle
31st March, 2023 to 27th April, 2023	3,189.95	3,272.95	3,070.25	3,187.95	3,188.00	Bearish
28th April, 2023 to 25th May, 2023	3,200.40	3,327.95	3,173.15	3,293.50	3,295.00	Bullish
26th May, 2023 to 29th June, 2023	3,293.50	3,372.00	3,156.00	3,215.45	3,221.00	Bearish
30th June, 2023 to 27th July, 2023	3,220.00	3,549.90	3,214.10	3,396.90	3398.00	Bullish
28th July, 2023 to 31st August, 2023	3385.00	3489.95	3331	3356.80	3361	Bearish
1st September, 2023 to 28th September, 2023	3366	3633.75	3356.80	3536.75	3549	Bullish
29th September 2023 to 26th October 2023	3537.20	3679	3330	3336.75	3331.80	Bearish
27th October, 2023 to 30th October, 2023	3350	3544	3311	3487.60	3487.90	Bullish
1st December, 2023 to 28th December, 2023	3500	3920	3490.05	3799.90	3796.15	Bullish
29th December, 2023 to 25th January, 2024	3792	3965	3651	3810.30	3807	Bullish
26th January, 2024 to 29th February, 2024	3800.80	4184.75	3780.85	4095.10	4113	Bullish
1st March, 2024 to 28th March, 2024	4107.20	4254.75	3829.40	3876.30	3882.10	Bearish
29th March, 2024 to 25th April, 2024	3897.70	4064.20	3800.90	3852.20	3851	Bearish
26th April, 2024 to 30th May, 2024	3855.15	3988	3715.45	3736.10	3739	Bearish
31st May, 2024 to 27th June, 2024	3740	3942	3591.50	3934.15	3928	Bullish
28th June, 2024 to 25th July, 2024	3917.80	4361.70	3884	4322.50	4332.25	Bullish

TCS 16- Month Back Test with Stop Loss

Month	Purchase Price	Target	Stop Loss	Amount	Target Date	Stop Loss Date	Profit	Loss
31st March, 2023 to 27th April, 2023	0	0	0	0	0	0	0	0
28th April, 2023 to 25th May, 2023	3295.00	3393.85	3173.15	100	0	16th June 2023	0	12185
26th May, 2023 to 29th June, 2023	0	0	0	0	0	0	0	0
30th June, 2023 to 27th July, 2023	3398.00	3499.94	3214.10	100	0	0	0	0
28th July, 2023 to 31st August, 2023	0	0	0	0	0	0	0	3700
1st September, 2023 to 28th September, 2023	3549.00	3655.47	3356.80	100	9th October 2023	0	10647	0
29th September 2023 to 26th October 2023	0	0	0	0	0	0	0	0
27th October, 2023 to 30th November, 2023	3487.90	3592.54	3311.00	100	6th December 2023	0	10464	0
1st December, 2023 to 28th December, 2023	3796.15	3910.03	3490.05	100	15th January 2024	0	11388	0

29th December, 2023 to 25th January, 2024	3807.00	3921.21	3651.00	100	2nd February 2024	0	11421	0
26th January, 2024 to 29th February, 2024	4113.00	4236.39	3780.85	100	13th March 2024	0	12339	0
1st March, 2024 to 28th March, 2024	0	0	0	0	0	0	0	0
29th March, 2024 to 25th April, 2024	0	0	0	0	0	0	0	0
26th April, 2025 to 30th May, 2024	0	0	0	0	0	0	0	
31st May, 2024 to 27th June, 2024	3928.00	4045.84	3591.50	100	4th July 2024	0	11784	
28th June, 2024 to 25th July, 2024	4332.25	4462.22	3884.00	100	19th August 2024	0	12997	
						TOTAL	81040	15885
					Net Profit	65155		

and when a new bullish candle is formed, the price has fallen by more than 3.14 per cent from the previous purchase price, and they have the ability to buy for averaging, they should use it without a stop loss. Now whether to keep a stop loss or not, this decision should be taken purely at your own discretion.

Let us see the result without stop loss in the following table-

You can see from the above table that you did not have to do averaging even once and the profit was booked, albeit with a slight delay, and you would have made a profit of ₹ 1,01,119 in the last 16 months without brokerage and charges.

Now you can argue that this was a bull market; what would have happened if it was a bearish market? Actually, our subconscious mind does not accept that we can earn money by trading in the stock market. That is why you make such arguments as what would have happened in a bearish market? You can do this kind of research yourself and see the results.

After all, the capital is yours and you have to decide on any type of trade based on your risk profile and the advice of your investment advisor. The book can give you an idea. You are free to do your own research. You can watch the video of this method in my 'Mahesh Kaushik Ki Pathshala' series in Class 6 Technical Analysis. After the release of the above video, another channel on YouTube, which belongs to Mr. Nitin Potade, has also created and shared an automatic Google Finance Sheet on his channel to do its back test on any stock. You can also take the help of his sheet to do the back test.

TCS 16- Month Back Test without Stop Loss

Month	Purchase Price	Target	Stop Loss	Amount	Target Date	Stop Loss Date	Profit	Loss
31st March, 2023 to 27th April, 2023	0	0	0	0	0	0	0	0
28th April, 2023 to 25th May, 2023	3,295.00	3,393.85	0	100	14, July, 2023	0	9,858	0
26th May, 2023 to 29th June, 2023	0	0	0	0	0	0	0	0
30th June, 2023 to 27th July, 2023	3,398.00	3,499.94	3,214.10	100	12, September, 2023	0	10,194	0
28th July, 2023 to 31st August, 2023	0	0	0	0	0	0	0	0
1st Sept, 2023 to 28th Sept, 2023	3,549.00	3,655.47	3,356.80	100	9, October, 2023	0	10,647	0
29th September 2023 to 26th October 2023	0	0	0	0	0	0	0	0
27th October, 2023 to 30th Nov, 2023	3,487.90	3,592.54	3,311.00	100	6, December, 2023	0	10,464	0
1st Dec, 2023 to 28th Dec, 2023	3,796.15	3,910.03	3,490.05	100	15, January, 2024	0	11,388	0
29th December, 2023 to 25th January, 2024	3,807.00	3,921.21	3,651.00	100	02, February, 2024	0	11,421	0
26th January, 2024 to 29th February, 2024	4,113.00	4,236.39	3,780.85	100	13, March, 2024	0	12,339	0
1st March, 2024 to 28th March, 2024	0	0	0	0	0	0	0	0
29th March, 2024 to 25th April, 2024	0	0	0	0	0	0	0	0
26th April, 2024 to 30th May, 2024	0	0	0	0	0	0	0	0
31st May, 2024 to 27th June, 2024	3,928.00	4,045.84	3,591.50	100	4, July, 2024	0	11,784	0
28th June, 2024 to 25th July, 2024	4,332.25	4,462.22	3,884.00	100	19, August, 2024	0	12,997	0
						Total	1,01,119	0
					Net Profit	1,01,119		

5

Simplest Trading System based on Support and Resistance in Technical Analysis

It is very important to identify support and resistance in technical analysis. Support and resistance are two such magical points that whether you know anything or not, if you just know about support and resistance, then you can earn a lot of money by trading with them.

It is possible that you are an old trader. It is also possible that you have done heavy courses on technical analysis and after reading the above line, you are thinking that it is not possible to earn money with the help of only two points (support and resistance). Actually, our ego is our biggest enemy. When we lose money in some trades, then our ego tries to make us believe that -

1. It is very difficult to earn money in the stock market.
2. There is a secret method to earn money, which is very hard. One will have to learn it.

After that, we get lost in endless search. We buy big books, watch long videos; even then when we cannot make money, we attend seminars by paying huge amounts and buy paid courses. After that, the names of various chart patterns keep crowding our mind.

We consider ourselves experts once again and try to take big trades. Even then when we cannot make money, our ego says, "The stock market is a gamble. No one can make money in it".

But I would like to remind you of the famous novelist, Oscar Wilde's quote-

"*Life is not complex; we are complex.*

Life is simple and the simple thing is the right thing".

If I write this in my stock market language, it means that "Trading is not complex. Our mind likes complexity. Trading is simple and ordinary and simple things are right".

There was an aircraft engineer named Kelly Johnson. He gave 'The Kiss Principle', according to which, 'Keep it simple, stupid' or 'Keep it sweet and simple'. This principle means that there is no need to make very complicated machines to make an airplane. If you keep it simple and stupid, then also the plane will be made.

With time, his statement proved to be correct. After that, a simple plane like a drone was made. Nowadays, even the children's helicopter available in shops for ₹ 100 can fly a short distance like a real helicopter.

Therefore, the method I will tell you will enable you to fly in the stock market even with just support resistance. But keep the flight short. Do not forget that "even the best plane can crash".

Now, without preaching too much let me start giving you knowledge of this simplest method. For this also, instead of using any chart software, I will use free charts and free data available on the BSE website.

To explain the method of support resistance, I have taken the example of Kotak Mahindra Bank share data from February 2024 to July 2024. Let us see what would have happened if we had taken out the support resistance and taken trade in it in the months of March, April, June and July?

First of all, if we have to take a trade in March 2024, then for this we will have to see the chart of February 2024.

Now I already know the thought that is coming in your mind—why are we taking calendar month here? You may ask that I have already told you in this book that if we take the month as per the expiry of future option then the results are better. This is absolutely correct. But I want to keep this chapter simple and stupid as per the Kiss Principle. So I have taken the calendar month to keep the month simple, so that you can understand the simplicity of this method.

So the chart from 1st February, 2024 to 29th February, 2024 would look like this. Here the close price of 2nd February, 2024 was 1,824.00 (on BSE), which is the highest level of this chart and the lowest level of the chart is the close price of 28th February, 2024 at 1,683.55 (on BSE).

Chart of Kotak Mahindra Bank for March 24

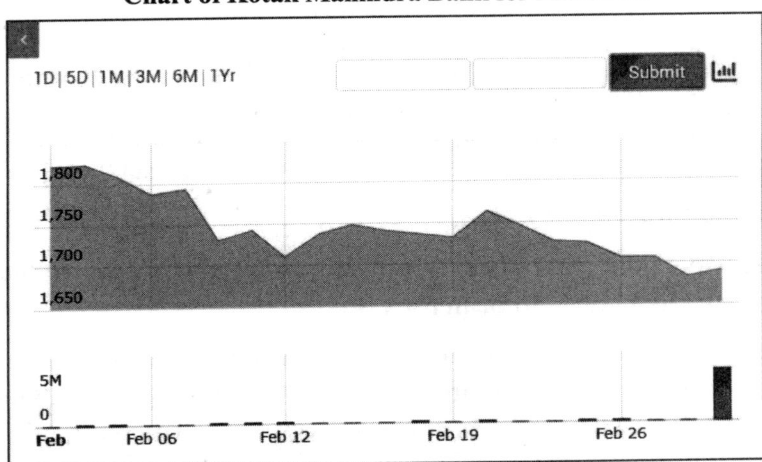

The point to be noted here is that I have used the close price. On the chart, only the close price is given importance. To show this, I have shown you how to find support and resistance from the chart; otherwise, if I had told you how to find it directly from the historical data of the stock, then you would not have understood why I have taken the close price instead of giving importance to the highest and lowest level of the month.

So what do you understand here?

The highest close of the month is the resistance of the stock. The lowest close of the month is the support of the stock. That is, if we have to trade in Kotak Mahindra Bank in March 2024, then we will consider closing above the highest level of February 2024, i.e. 1,824, as breaking of the resistance. In other words, if the stock manages to close above 1,824 in March 2024, then we will consider it as a bullish signal for the next trading day and to use it in the trade; we can buy shares in the cash market. If you are very greedy, then you can buy shares on margin. Those who are experienced traders with high net worth can take positions in futures, buy calls, sell puts, etc.

Whatever you do, always do it keeping in mind your risk profile and remember that no method is 100 per cent perfect in the stock market and if the stock closes above the resistance, there is no guarantee that it will not fall back.

That is why I always give importance to buying in cash; so that those who do not keep a stop loss can also exit by averaging it forward (average will also be based on closing above the resistance).

So the safest thing is that -

1. Always take trades based on technical analysis only in blue chip stocks like Nifty 50 or Sensex 30.
2. If you do not keep a stop loss, if one breakout fails, then keep capital of at least five trades to buy again for averaging on the second breakout. (More than five is good. Here, five is the minimum.)
3. If the stock closes above a resistance point and then falls again, and then closes above the resistance point again in the following months, then to buy for averaging, keep in mind that this price (the price of closing above the resistance again) must be at least 3.14 per cent below your last purchase price. This 3.14 per cent is the value of π, which will be explained further in the chapter titled 'My Research on the Physics of the Stock Market'.

Similarly, if the stock closes below the lowest close of the previous month, it will be considered as a support break. If the previous position is in profit, you can book profit on this. If the previous position is in loss and you are a trader who keeps a stop loss, then you can consider it as a stop loss.

Traders with high net worth and high experience, who do short selling, buy puts, sell calls, etc., can use it for this.

Now, without showing you the chart, I will directly explain to you what happened in March 2024 on the basis of data. Even if you do not understand the above theoretical facts, if you understand this back test, then everything will be clear.

See the data of Kotak Mahindra Bank for March 2024 in the following figure.

Price Data of Kotak Mahindra Bank for March 2024 (BSE)

Date	Open	High	Low	Close
01/3/2024	1,691.05	1,729.90	1,691.05	1,727.25
02/3/2024	1,727.00	1,732.60	1,720.00	1,724.65
04/3/2024	1,725.45	1,741.55	1,718.50	1,727.00
05/3/2024	1,720.50	1,726.95	1,708.95	1,716.00
06/3/2024	1,720.65	1,771.30	1,719.00	1,758.30
07/3/2024	1,760.00	1,764.90	1,744.25	1,748.15
11/3/2024	1,755.40	1,764.85	1,725.00	1,729.20
12/3/2024	1,734.00	1,742.85	1,708.15	1,720.35
13/3/2024	1,721.05	1,742.45	1,717.85	1,727.90
14/3/2024	1,725.00	1,757.55	1,720.00	1,743.15
15/3/2024	1,739.40	1,755.00	1,721.50	1,738.95
18/3/2024	1,739.65	1,744.90	1,715.40	1,737.25
19/3/2024	1,738.80	1,756.95	1,731.30	1,748.85
20/3/2024	1,749.05	1,768.60	1,730.55	1,765.25
21/3/2024	1,774.35	1,790.00	1,765.25	1,772.20
22/3/2024	1,760.70	1,782.85	1,760.70	1,774.70
26/3/2024	1,771.75	1,775.25	1,750.00	1,754.95
27/3/2024	1,755.00	1,778.90	1,752.95	1,775.65
28/3/2024	1,776.15	1,803.50	1,774.10	1,785.80

In this you can see that in the entire month, neither did the stock close above the resistance of 1,824 (highest close of previous month) nor below the support of 1,683.55 (lowest close of previous month); hence, the stock remained sideways in March 2024. There was neither any opportunity to buy nor any opportunity to sell.

But now our support and resistance will change for the next month. Now we will consider the highest close of this month, 1,785.80, as the resistance of the next month and the lowest close of this month, 1,716.00, as the support of the next month.

See the Kotak Mahindra Bank data for April 2024 in the following figure.

Price Data of Kotak Mahindra Bank for April 2024 (BSE)

Date	Open	High	Low	Close
01/4/2024	1,790.10	1,817.70	1,786.15	1,789.50
02/4/2024	1,794.90	1,795.45	1,754.90	1,756.65
03/4/2024	1,755.95	1,755.95	1,729.30	1,731.50
04/4/2024	1,740.00	1,751.85	1,723.40	1,748.70
05/4/2024	1,748.00	1,787.40	1,741.30	1,785.25
08/4/2024	1,798.95	1,801.20	1,784.75	1,788.00
09/4/2024	1,791.00	1,793.00	1,776.10	1,782.25
10/4/2024	1,787.80	1,829.25	1,783.25	1,825.10
12/4/2024	1,818.65	1,818.65	1,798.75	1,813.60
15/4/2024	1,777.35	1,809.00	1,777.35	1,797.85
16/4/2024	1,775.05	1,804.60	1,775.05	1,795.40
18/4/2024	1,797.80	1,813.10	1,782.80	1,786.45
19/4/2024	1,776.00	1,804.95	1,763.40	1,793.20
22/4/2024	1,800.20	1,822.00	1,800.20	1,809.85
23/4/2024	1,819.75	1,828.90	1,803.80	1,813.25
24/4/2024	1,806.65	1,845.50	1,806.65	1,843.05
25/4/2024	1,675.00	1,689.45	1,620.00	1,643.00
26/4/2024	1,644.00	1,654.80	1,605.00	1,608.40
29/4/2024	1,613.20	1,646.95	1,609.40	1,640.25
30/4/2024	1,643.70	1,647.00	1,621.00	1,623.75

In this you can see that on 1st April,2024, the stock closed above the resistance of 1,785.80 at 1,789.50. Next day, on 2nd April, 2024, you could have easily bought it at the previous day's close price of 1,789.50.

As I said, for short term trading, it is best to keep the target approximately equal to the value of pi, i.e. 3 per cent.

Your stop loss for this purchase would have been the previous month's low level or support level of ₹ 1,716.

You can see in the above data that before this stop loss was hit, you got a 3 per cent upside target of 1,789.50 at 1,843.18 on 24th April, 2024.

After this, on 25th April, 2024, the stock opened below last month's support of 1,716 at 1675 and if you had done short selling due to breaking of support, then you can see that you would have got a target of up to 4 per cent on the downside, because the stock had also made a low of 1,605 on 26th April,2024.

If you extract support and resistance for next month's trade from the above data for the month of April, they would be as follows—

1. Support - Lowest close price of April - 1,608.40
2. Resistance - Highest close price of April - 1,843.05

Now let us look at the data for May 2024.

Price Data of Kotak Mahindra Bank for May 2024 (BSE)

Date	Open	High	Low	Close
02/5/2024	1,596.00	1,596.00	1,552.55	1,575.80
03/5/2024	1,584.65	1,587.30	1,544.15	1,547.25
06/5/2024	1,600.00	1,633.00	1,595.15	1,624.75
07/5/2024	1,630.00	1,647.00	1,617.30	1,644.30
08/5/2024	1,640.00	1,657.00	1,635.35	1,648.60
09/5/2024	1,648.35	1,661.55	1,636.50	1,642.25
10/5/2024	1,644.00	1,653.05	1,615.75	1,630.50
13/5/2024	1,624.95	1,644.25	1,615.35	1,641.15
14/5/2024	1,640.25	1,649.80	1,633.00	1,646.10
15/5/2024	1,643.30	1,654.00	1,637.30	1,651.25
16/5/2024	1,652.05	1,675.00	1,648.10	1,671.90
17/5/2024	1,663.15	1,705.95	1,663.15	1,697.00
18/5/2024	1,690.05	1,702.00	1,689.15	1,696.40
21/5/2024	1,696.40	1,714.60	1,691.00	1,697.10
22/5/2024	1,707.00	1,707.00	1,681.05	1,700.40
23/5/2024	1,700.45	1,712.95	1,697.70	1,708.65
24/5/2024	1,700.15	1,717.75	1,694.55	1,703.00
27/5/2024	1,701.05	1,721.90	1,701.05	1,710.95
28/5/2024	1,719.85	1,719.85	1,699.50	1,702.25
29/5/2024	1,692.05	1,710.45	1,682.05	1,688.30
30/5/2024	1,680.25	1,707.35	1,680.25	1,690.65
31/5/2024	1,695.05	1,703.65	1,661.75	1,679.70

You can see that on 2nd May, 2024, the stock opened below the support of 1,608.40 at 1,596 and had you sold short based on its opening below the support at 1,596, you would have easily got a 3 per cent downside target of 1,548.12 on 3rd May, 2024, when the stock made a low of 1,544.15. You will be amazed to see throughout this chapter how the value of pi, approximately 3.14, fits so well here!

If you could not book this profit, you should have closed the short position on 6th May, 2024, when the stock closed back above the support at 1,608.40.

Some traders buy after taking stock going below the support and closing back above the support as a bullish signal, which is fine. If you had bought at the closing price of 1,624.75 on 6th May, 2024, you could have easily got a target of up to (?) per cent. However, in this type of trading, a target of 3 per cent is good.

So what did you understand from this?

Two types of breakouts are considered for buying –

1. Closing above the resistance at least.
2. Closing above the support after closing below the support for two days is also considered a type of breakout.

Similarly, there are two types of negative breakouts considered for selling—

1. Closing below support.
2. Closing below resistance after closing above resistance for at least two days.

Let us continue the learning process and find support and resistance for trading in June 2024 based on the above data.

1. Support— Lowest close of May 2024 - 1,547.95
2. Resistance— Highest close of May 2024 - 1,710.95

Now look at the data for June 2024—

Price Data of Kotak Mahindra Bank for June 2024 (BSE)

Date	Open	High	Low	Close
03/6/2024	1,720.00	1,736.60	1,700.45	1,719.05
04/6/2024	1,718.00	1,718.00	1,602.20	1,638.60
05/6/2024	1,667.75	1,724.70	1,645.40	1,718.75
06/6/2024	1.727.95	1,738.00	1,703.95	1,735.00
07/6/2024	1,734.95	1,758.60	1,721.85	1,753.05
10/6/2024	1,759.95	1,772.95	1,733.30	1,745.50
11/6/2024	1,745.30	1,745.50	1,717.10	1,720.30
12/6/2024	1,716.10	1,733.90	1,711.65	1,715.50
13/6/2024	1,730.00	1,737.80	1,719.05	1,726.40
14/6/2024	1,711.15	1,735.00	1,711.00	1,717.00
18/6/2024	1,717.20	1,723.95	1,703.50	1,719.60
19/6/2024	1,728.20	1,763.00	1,716.00	1,748.25
20/6/2024	1,757.00	1,789.90	1,757.00	1,765.05
21/6/2024	1,765.10	1,787.00	1,745.50	1,773.50
24/6/2024	1,759.35	1,775.95	1,749.80	1,772.40
25/6/2024	1,773.05	1,797.90	1,763.50	1,782.15
26/6/2024	1,782.70	1,815.70	1,776.75	1,797.10
27/6/2024	1,795.50	1,837.85	1,785.25	1,830.80
28/6/2024	1,815.65	1,847.50	1,799.00	1,803.00

Here, by closing above the resistance on 3rd June, 2024, you could have bought the next day at the close price of 1,719.05.

Now many new readers will raise the question here that the level of 1,719.05 was not formed the next day. It opened at 1,718 and remained below it throughout the day.

So keep in mind that we are talking about buying here, not selling. That is, if you place a limit order at 1,719.05, then that limit order can be executed at a price below that. That is, you would have got shares at 1,718 instead of 1,719.05 as soon as the market opened.

Now, some people will say that the stock closed below the resistance (1,710.95) on 4th June, 2024, so has it become a negative breakout?

No, read the rules I mentioned above carefully. If the price closes above the resistance once and then closes below the resistance for at least two days, then only it should be considered a negative breakout. Hence, on 5th June, 2024, it closed back at 1,718.75.

So you see, how simple it is! No chart pattern, no candlestick, yet you can trade so easily with just support and resistance! If you want, you can keep a stop loss as mentioned above and if you are investing only in the top 10 large cap companies with less than your own capital, as mentioned in the previous chapter, and whenever the resistance is about to break, at that time, if the previous position is held but profit is not booked and if a breakout occurs, then if the price at that time has fallen by more than 3.14 per cent from your previous purchase price, and if you have the ability to buy for averaging, then you should use it without a stop loss. Now whether to keep a stop loss or not, this decision should be taken purely at your own discretion.

If I demonstrate a long back test in this book, the readers will get bored and the book will also become longer than necessary. But you should try this method in the above mentioned way of back testing on the top 10 market cap companies as well as all the companies of Nifty 50 on at least one year of data in both bearish and bullish market conditions. Then you will become so perfect in identifying support and resistance that you will be able to guess by just looking at any stock whether it should be bought now or not.

❑

6

Trading by Bearish Candle Being Formed Using the Honma Genius Method

In the first chapter of this book, I introduced you to 'The God of Markets'. If you have forgotten it, let me remind you once again. Munehisa Honma was born in 1724 in Sakata city of Japan. Munehisa Honma is also known by his other name, 'Sokyu Honma'.

The world's first future market was started in Japan in 1710, in which future prices of rice were traded through coupons.

From that time, Sokyu Honma was a rice trader and by trading in rice, he earned so much money till 1755, which was equal to 10 billion dollars today.

That is why, in history, there has been no successful trader like Munehisa Honma till date. This is the reason why he is also known in history as 'The God of Markets'. It was Munehisa Honma who wrote a book for traders in Japanese language in 1755, named 'San-en-kinsen'. Its English translation is also known as 'The Fountain of Gold - The Three Monkey Record of Money'.

The principles described by Munehisa Honma in this book later became the basis of candlestick charting.

You will be surprised to know that Sokyu Honma has not mentioned candlestick charts anywhere in this book. Even so, in candlestick charts, we basically predict the market movement from the psychology of the market. Understanding the psychology of the market is the key to technical analysis techniques around the world.

In the previous chapters, you understood how you can easily make money by buying when a monthly bullish candle is formed. But if you read the above book by Honma, you find that he was in favour of buying when the market is falling and by buying on a bullish candle, we are doing exactly the opposite. Also, he used to say to wait for at least 3 days to gauge the market situation; but in the above method, we have used data of about 30 days.

Actually, it is more convenient to trade along with the direction of the market, so people started using bullish candles for buying and since 1755, no one has paid much attention to make a trading method from his book. Presently, in 2024, I have modified his method according to the current context and invented the Honma Genius Method, in which you buy on bearish candles.

I have taken his method a little further, where you do not need any software to make a candlestick chart. You can check in Excel whether this week's candle is a bearish candle or a bullish candle. I have made some good improvements in it and researching stock market data is my hobby. I have invented many methods of successful swing trading in stocks. That is why my followers call me 'Share Genius'. So how did I name this method? I took the name 'Honma' from Munehisa Honma's name and took the word 'genius' from my name, 'Share Genius' and combined 'Honma' and 'genius' to name this method, the 'Honma Genius Method'. So all of you can use this 'Honma Genius Method'.

What is the fundamental difference between the method of buying on a bullish candle described in the previous chapter and the method of buying on a bearish candle described in this chapter? Always remember that "buying shares should always be done only when a bullish candle is formed" because if you keep buying on a bearish candle, it is possible that the share may go into the bearish zone for a long time or some fundamental change may take place in it, due to which it may continue to fall for a long time. Then most of your capital may get stuck. If you want to buy a falling share, then for this I have a method based on RSI, which will be explained in the subsequent chapters.

If you use ETF instead of shares, then ETF is not a single share. ETF stands for **Exchange Traded Fund**. It is like a mutual fund which has a lot of shares, but these shares are traded in the market, just like any share. So, while trading in ETF, if you buy a falling ETF even on a bearish candle, then you buy a whole portfolio, in which if one stock falls, there are chances the other can rise. So, there is a full possibility of a bounce back for trading when the market condition improves. That is why "buying in ETF should always be done when a bearish candle is formed."

You will enjoy learning this method and you will realise how easy it is to earn money in the stock market without stop loss! Whether the market is in a bull run or a bear run, everything is practical. We will explain it with examples. So, let us start learning this method immediately.

To explain this method, I will use the most voluminous Nifty BeES ETF based on Nifty 50. We will not use it in Nifty futures or intraday, as we do not place any stop loss in this method. Hence, ETFs in cash segment are safe for us. After all, when our aim is to earn money by trading, we do not need to go into futures or options when we can take full advantage of Nifty fluctuations by trading in Nifty BeES ETF. We do not need to go into intraday either.

You can trade in this ETF like shares. It has 50 stocks of Nifty 50. This ETF holds all the 50 stocks of Nifty 50 in the same proportion as Nifty. So if we track Nifty BeES and trade in Nifty BeES, we can take full advantage of trading in Nifty. Also, we can buy it in cash in delivery. Most of the readers here already know these facts, yet they want to trade in intraday or futures instead of cash. Why is it so?

In intraday or futures they get the benefit of leverage. If they invest ₹ 1 lakh in a share and trade ₹ 10 lakh, then they get the benefit of leverage. But due to the large lot size and fixed time period, you are forced to keep a stop loss and you may also have to bear a big loss. So, I say do not use such huge leverage which requires stop loss. If you want to use leverage, then instead of intraday or futures option, you can use it in MTF trading i.e., margin funding trading, where you can keep small lot size as per your capacity and can hold the position for almost a year by paying a little interest.

Rules of Honma Genius Method –

1. It should be used only in ETFs based on Nifty, Bank Nifty, Nifty Next 50, Nifty Midcap Select and Nifty Financial Services, Sensex etc., which have high volume, i.e., have decent volume most of the days.
2. Since the ETF is based on some selected index, this method will be implemented by creating weekly candles based on the weekly expiry of these futures options. Hence, I recommend selecting exchange traded funds based on such indexes which trade weekly in futures options.
3. We will select the week based on expiry only for making candles; but we will take position in cash or MTF (margin) only. Since stop loss is not used in this method and there is a need to buy repeatedly on bearish candles every week like a Systematic Investment Plan (SIP), this method is not suitable for future option trading.
4. In this method, we have to check how the candle is formed every week (week taken on the basis of expiry of future option) and whenever a bearish candle is formed, we have to buy at that time.
5. You can also make this purchase on the basis of the method mentioned in chapter 3, by considering the price prevailing in the last half hour on the day of expiry as the close price and making a candle based on that. Those who do not wish to do this can also buy at the previous day's close price on the first day of the new series.
6. As I have mentioned earlier, for trading, it is best to keep a profit target equal to the value of π, i.e., 3.14 per cent, or 3 per cent and those who do not wish to trade frequently and want slightly better returns can keep a target up to 6.28 per cent or 9.42 per cent (equivalent to 2 π or 3 π), but a profit target of 3per cent is the most suitable and is more likely to be achieved sooner.

Now, since you buy on every bearish candle, the target here is 3 per cent of the average price.

You can back test this method on the historical data of ETFs on any index that trades in futures.

I have back tested it on the historical data of Nifty BeES ETF from 1st January, 2024 to 21st June, 2024, in which, every week, whenever a bearish candle is formed, buy and whenever a bullish candle is formed, do not buy that week.

I think this system is completely opposite to your knowledge, because till date, you have learnt to buy when a bullish candle is formed and sell when a bearish candle is formed. This is true in the context of shares, but when you buy ETF, it is a type of mutual fund, in which if you make small weekly purchases, like SIP in shares, on every bearish candle, then when the index bounces back, you get the benefit of swing trading. For example, see the data of Nifty BeES from 29th December, 2023 to 25th January, 2024 in the following picture –

Nifty BeES Historical Data

Date	OPEN	HIGH	LOW	close	Candle Formation	Buy Quantity	investment with brokerage	Total Quantity	Total Investment	Average Price	Target 3 %
29-Dec-23	247.35	247.35	238	239.65							
1-Jan-24	240.99	241.14	238.01	240.35							
2-Jan-24	241	241	238	239.21							
3-Jan-24	240	240	237.5	237.74							
4-Jan-24	237.7	239.59	237.19	239.3	Bearish Candle	42	10070.70	42	10070.70	239.78	246.97
5-Jan-24	239.8	240	238.01	239.74							
8-Jan-24	242	242	237.5	237.68							
9-Jan-24	239.99	239.99	237.5	237.78							
10-Jan-24	238.99	238.99	236.76	238.76							
11-Jan-24	239.7	239.7	238.01	238.87	Bearish Candle	42	10052.61	84	20123.31	239.56	246.75
12-Jan-24	239.01	242.35	239.01	241.73							
15-Jan-24	241.73	244.3	241.73	244.07							
16-Jan-24	244.6	244.99	242.41	243.24							
17-Jan-24	240.99	243	238.1	238.38							
18-Jan-24	237.99	238.21	233.3	237.51	Bearish Candle	42	9995.37	126	30118.68	239.04	246.21
19-Jan-24	239.99	239.99	237.75	239.15							
20-Jan-24	246.3	246.3	238.5	238.73	When Open=High we are not able to book profit because sometime						
23-Jan-24	241.9	241.9	234.5	234.87	ETF opens high but most of the orders are not executed at this price						
24-Jan-24	235.68	237.59	233.5	237.29							
25-Jan-24	238	238	235.1	236.15	Bearish Candle	42	9938.14	168	40056.81	238.43	245.59

You can see that here in the week from 29th December 2023 to 4th January 2024, a bearish candle was formed due to the close price (weekly close) being lower than the open price (weekly open) and the estimated purchase of ₹ 10,000 is considered to be around the close price in the last half hour of Thursday every week.

So, in this way, in the above four weeks data you saw that on 20th January, 2024, the open price was 246.30, more than our target of 246.21; but I did not consider profit to be booked here, because I believe - 'Honesty is the best policy'. Therefore, I did not consider profit to be booked here, because when the open price is equal to the high price, most people do not get the opportunity to book profit.

You can see the data of this back test from 29th January, 2024 to 22nd February, 2024 in the following figure—

Honma Genius Method Back Test Data

Date	OPEN	HIGH	LOW	close	Candle Formation	Buy Quantity	investment with brokerage	Total Quantity	Total Investment	Average Price	Target 3 %
29-Jan-24	238	240.4	236.15	240.05							
30-Jan-24	241.99	241.99	237.95	238.13							
31-Jan-24	238.78	240.48	237.5	240.26							
1-Feb-24	241.99	241.99	239.48	240.03	Bullish Candle						
2-Feb-24	243.4	244.28	240.01	241.3							
5-Feb-24	248.55	248.55	239.9	240.24	When Open=High we are not able to book profit because sometime ETF						
6-Feb-24	247.45	247.45	237.65	242.01	opens high but most of the orders are not executed at this price						
7-Feb-24	249.25	249.25	234.75	242.35							
8-Feb-24	242.35	243.38	239.9	240.28	Bearish Candle	42	10111.94	210	50168.76	238.90	246.07
9-Feb-24	240.9	241.02	239	240.78							
12-Feb-24	241	242.5	238.97	239.32							
13-Feb-24	246.5	246.5	238.7	240.59	When Open=High we are not able to book profit because sometime ETF						
14-Feb-24	239.9	241.99	237.55	241.55	opens high but most of the orders are not executed at this price						
15-Feb-24	242.99	243	241.2	242.72	Bullish Candle						
16-Feb-24	244	244.23	242.58	243.99							
19-Feb-24	244.5	245.75	243.58	245.04							
20-Feb-24	246.99	246.99	243.01	245.37							
21-Feb-24	246	246.29	243.5	243.87							
22-Feb-24	244.5	246.21	242.45	245.79	Bullish Candle						

You can see that here also there were opportunities to book profit from 5th February, 2024 to 13th February, 2024; but here also, profit was not considered to be booked as the open price was equal to the high price and on 21st February, 2024, a profit of ₹ 1,505 is considered to be booked with a target of 3 per cent.

You can see the complete data of this back test on my Youtube channel by searching the video named 'Honma Genius method', which gives regular income without stop loss in Nifty Bank Nifty.

If you do not want to average out at the same price again and again in this method, then you can also make a correction in it that you do not average out until the price is less than 3.14 per cent from your last purchase on the formation of a bearish candle.

This will save you from averaging again and again and you will not invest more money in sideways and bearish market.

If you use this method in ETFs in indices traded in all the future options mentioned in this chapter and buy only when there is a difference of at least 3.14 per cent in the price from the last purchase, then you can easily book profit from time to time in different ETFs by averaging less frequently. This method is not for people with a trader mentality. It is for those who want to earn regular income with safe investment. Risk is present in all the methods of the stock market, but in this, there is a little less risk in trading in ETF.

❑

7

How to Trade by Super Breakout Method?

If you have bought this book thinking that I will teach you by showing you pictures of candlestick chart patterns, telling you their Japanese names, that this is a Try Star pattern, this is a Breakaway pattern, this is a Double Top, this is a Double Bottom, do this in this, do that in this, then you may be disappointed, because thousands of books have been written all over the world on this type of technical analysis, which, in my opinion, do not give practical results most of the time in the current circumstances when algo trading is done.

If you want to learn the names of these types of chart patterns and what happens when they are formed, then type 'Free Technical Analysis Books PDF' on Google. You will get many such PDF books to read for free. But in this book, I will focus on telling you the practical methods that I have discovered on the basis of my own research.

One such method of mine, Super Breakout, has been appreciated by traders all over the world. The accuracy of this method is getting the most appreciation through the comments on my YouTube channel and emails. Therefore, I am going to explain this method to you in the upcoming chapters.

Please do not get confused by the simplicity of this method, because I have already told you about the relevance of simplicity in chapter 5 through the famous quote of novelist Oscar Wilde who had said, *"Life is not complex, we are complex. Life is simple and the simple thing is the right thing".*

Keeping facts in mind, the simplest indicator of technical analysis; the 'Simple Moving Average', is going to be used in this method as well. Here, at some places, I have also written 'Simple Moving Average' as 'Daily Moving Average'. Both are the same.

Let us start learning the Super Breakout method. Take the 5 DMA, 10 DMA, 15 DMA, 50 DMA, 100 DMA and 200 DMA of a stock. You can see these six simple moving averages for free on various screener websites and in the charts provided by your broker. You can calculate them yourself in Excel or by entering the formula in Google Finance Sheet. I have given a link named 'Super Breakout Stocks' on my blog, *'MaheshchandraKaushik.com'*; there you will also get the link of its Google Finance Sheet.

Now, what is left to do? You have to find a stock whose current market price is above its 5 DMA, 10 DMA, 15 DMA, 50 DMA, 100 DMA but below 200 DMA.

The Google Finance Sheet I have created for this purpose finds such a stock by calculating with the help of a formula. You can also create such a screener on screener sites.

Now what does a stock which has crossed the 5, 10, 15, 50, 100 day moving average but is still below the 200 day moving average indicate?

It indicates that the stock was falling for a long time because it is still below the 200 day moving average.

But the phase of decline in it is almost over because it has crossed the 5, 10, 15, 50, 100 day moving average.

Now as soon as such a stock crosses the 200 day moving average, it will cross all its moving averages of 5, 10, 15, 50, 100 and 200 day DMA. I have named this as 'Super Breakout'.

In this, when the stock crosses 5, 10, 15, 50 and 100 day DMA, but is still below 200 DMA, then a GTT order (Good Till Trigger Order) is placed for that stock at 200 DMA. As soon as the stock crosses 200

DMA, your GTT order is triggered and the stock is bought by your broker in your account.

I prefer to take a profit target of 6.28 per cent in such cases, because according to my research, the profit target of 6.28 per cent is likely to be achieved in most of the cases.

Here always remember this disclaimer that "**investment in stock market is always risky and invest only on the advice of your investment advisor based on your risk- taking capacity and your risk profile, because no method in stock market is 100 per cent perfect and there is no guarantee that you will get profit from it. The author of the book will not be responsible for any loss incurred due to any method mentioned in the book**".

Now, your question is natural that what to do if the stock falls back after crossing 200 DMA?

Actually, we do not trust any method. Our mind-set is filled with more loss than profit. That is why we always ask for stop loss, because we are afraid of the stock market.

My opinion in this is that if you want to keep a stop loss, you can keep the lowest price of the last 20 trading sessions as the stop loss; but I do not recommend dividing your capital into 500 parts and investing more than $1/50^{th}$ of the amount in one share of such super breakout stocks, so that if the stock goes above 200 DMA and comes back down, you can hold it for a few days. Only 1/50th of your capital will be blocked; with the remaining 49 parts, you can trade in other stocks using this method.

My own 18- year- old son has been using this method in his newly opened demat account for 6 months. In 6 months, he has booked a profit of more than 6.28 per cent in 80 per cent of the stocks he bought. The reason behind this 6.28 per cent profit is my compounding method of making ₹ 20 crores from ₹ 2 lakh, which is based on the mathematics of compounding. Later, I will also keep a chapter on this compounding so that you can get knowledge on compounding as well.

This method was liked by many traders. They repeatedly emailed me and asked me if this method can be used for the reverse, i.e., short selling?

So, for them, I have also made a reverse rule of this method that whenever the stock comes below its 5, 10, 15, 50, 100 day DMA but is still above 200 DMA, then such stock can be short sold if it is triggered below 200 DMA.

But here you must keep the highest price of the last 20 days as a stop loss. I do not recommend this type of short selling in intraday at all, because in intraday, even a small bounce of one day can bring you loss. Apart from intraday, in futures option etc. also, the use of stop loss is mandatory, due to which we are forced to book losses. So when our aim is to earn money, then instead of short selling, we can earn it by buying in cash.

For more information on the Super Breakout method, search for these two videos on my YouTube channel—

1. Identify stocks with the potential to rise and fall through Super Breakout.
2. Screener to select stocks with Super Breakout for intraday and swing trading.

This will give you a complete idea of the method.

In the next chapter, we will read about 'Consolidated Breakout', a method similar to Super Breakout.

❑

8

Trading by Consolidated Breakout

When I first made a video on consolidated dated breakout and informed the world about it, my followers were very upset. One of my followers commented, *"Mahesh Sir, these days your methods have become boring. The world is going into the 21st century and you are uploading videos on the same old moving average!"*

But after a few days, when people practically used this method, they understood its essence and how powerful this method is.

As I told you, this method is similar to super breakout, but in this, a signal to buy a stock is received even before the super breakout, meaning, in this method, we buy the stock before the 200 DMA is triggered in the super breakout, due to which profit booking is also done many times before the 200 DMA is reached.

But this does not reduce the importance of the Super Breakout method, because the probability of failure of the breakout in the Super Breakout method is less as compared to this method. Even so, the biggest advantage of the Consolidated Breakout method is that in the Super Breakout method, a GTT order has to be placed and when the 200 DMA changes with time, this GTT order has to be updated daily, which is a laborious job.

Many people do not want to work so hard. People consider the stock market to be an easy market for lazy people to earn money. But like any business, one has to work hard to earn money in this. The book that you are reading is also a type of hard work.

If the conditions of consolidated breakout are fulfilled, we can buy the stock at market price at any time and hold it for a profit target of 6.28 per cent.

Now, let me start explaining to you what consolidated breakout is.

1. In consolidated breakout, the stock which has made its 52-week low level should be considered, that is, look at the date of the stock making the 52- week high level and the date of it making the 52- week low level. If the date of making 52- week high level is around the date of your purchase, then it means that the stock is still falling from its 52-week high level. Considering such a stock for purchase may trap you at the higher level.

But if the 52- week low of the stock is near the date of your purchase, it means that the stock has touched its 52- week low and then consolidated and moved upwards. Hence, for consolidated dated breakout, only such stocks should be taken which have formed their 52- week low and then moved upwards.

After that, it has to be seen that the current market price (CMP) of the stock, 5 DMA, 20 DMA, 50 DMA, 100 DMA, 200 DMA do not have a difference of more than 5 per cent from each other.

That is, if all short term DMAs (of 5, 20 and 50 days) and all long term DMAs (of 100 and 200 days) have come within the range of 5per cent of the current market price, it means that the stock has consolidated enough and is about to give a breakout.

Understand its example. On 25th September, 2024, the share of Bandhan Bank was at a price of ₹ 205. Its 52-week high was 263.10, which it made on 4th January, 2024 and its 52-week low was 169.15, which it made on 4th June, 2024.

Now the nearest date to the current date, 25th September, 2024, is 4th June, 2024, when its lowest level was made, i.e., the first condition is fulfilled that the stock has come up after making its 52- week low.

Now its current price and all its DMAs are as follows –

CMP = 205

5 DMA = 211.04

20 DMA = 202.84

50 DMA = 201.19

100 DMA = 197.58

200 DMA = 204.40

All these DMAs are in the range of 5 per cent less or more than the current market price of the stock at ₹ 205, so considering it as a consolidated breakout, one can buy the stock at the current market price for a target of ₹ 6.28 per cent or ₹ 9.42per cent . I prefer the value of two π, i.e., 6.28 per cent. You will understand the reason for this in the subsequent chapters.

In the example of Bandhan Bank, the current market price was above 200 DMA; but it is not necessarily so. To understand this, look at another example of IndusInd Bank –

Price as on 25th September, 2024 = 1,441

5 DMA = 1,471.72

20 DMA = 1,444.91

50 DMA = 1,413.09

100 DMA = 1,436.78

200 DMA = 1,483.99

It made a 52-week high, 1,694.50, on 15th January, 2024 and a 52-week low 1,329.20, on 7th August, 2024. So the stock has consolidated from its 52- week low and all its 5, 20, 50, 100, 200 DMAs have come in the range of 5 per cent less or more than its current market price.

But here, the current market price is still below 200 DMA. You can also calculate consolidated breakout from Google Finance Sheets or create its screener as per your convenience.

You can copy the formula from the Google Finance Sheet mentioned by me or you can copy the entire sheet in your Google Drive with a new name.

You can also search and watch the video related to consolidated breakout that I have uploaded on YouTube. In the description of this video, you will also find the link of the Google Finance Sheet created by me, from where you can copy the sheet.

Overall, Super Breakout and Consolidated Breakout are similar. The main difference is that we can buy the stocks in Consolidated Breakout at their market price for holding in cash, while in Super Breakout, we have to place a GTT order for the 200 DMA to be triggered and update it daily according to the 200 DMA. Due to this, the Consolidated Breakout method is more suitable for those who are short of time and do not want to do so much hard work on a regular basis.

❑

9

Power of RSI

You must have often heard traders in the stock market talking about earning regular profits by taking trades based on RSI.

It is even said that about 95 per cent of traders in the world use RSI along with other indicators for their trading.

The full form of RSI is **'Relative Strength Index'**. It was invented by J. Welles Wilder in 1978; but even today most of the traders in our country do not understand the meaning of this simple indicator properly.

There are many different opinions in trading with RSI. Some say that trades should be bought and sold on reversal and an analyst like me will tell that when the stock is in the oversold zone, one should buy and when it is in the overbought zone, one should sell.

Actually, we want to bind this stock market to a fixed rule, which is not possible in the stock market.

In fact, science runs on rules; but stock market is not a science but an art. It is not possible to make any one rule for it, because art comes only from practise.

Now, as you know that in my writing style, I include some stories whenever it is relevant, so that you do not get bored of reading a difficult subject like technical analysis and you also easily get the message I want to give through the story.

In this context, my father, Late Shri Hiralal Kaushik, used to tell me the story of a physician in my childhood, which is perfectly apt in the context of RSI.

A person started working as a compounder with a physician to learn the physician's profession. A day before that, a feast had been organised in the village, after which most of the villagers complained of constipation after eating fried *puris* and potato dish.

So, it was a coincidence that as soon as the compounder joined the new job, the first patient who came to the physician suffered from constipation. The physician ordered the compounder to give him 2 *tolas* of *senna* decoction. Senna is a herb in Ayurveda, which is a laxative and the physician use it to treat constipation.

Now the second patient also came with constipation. The physician again ordered to give the same 2 tolas (approximately 20 ml) of senna decoction.

Now the villagers were suffering from constipation due to eating potatoes-puri in the feast, so that day, almost all the patients came with constipation and the physician gave the same medicine, 'senna decoction', to all.

This made the new servant that the physician had hired understand that practising medicine is very easy. The other colourful bottles that he had kept were just for show. That senna decoction is the medicine for every disease. So now there is no use in learning more. I have already learned everything I needed to learn.

That new compounder went to another village and started working as a physician. Now you can understand, whatever disease a patient came with to that new physician, he would give him senna decoction, due to which the patient would start suffering from diarrhoea.

An old man in the village even died due to severe diarrhoea. Now the villagers got angry with the new physician. They beat him up and drove him out of the village.

Overall, the gist of the story is that just like the same medicine does not work for all diseases, similarly the decision of buying and selling from the RSI indicator should also be taken according to the trader's mentality and his capital.

It is appropriate to take the decision based on experience like the old physician, and not to apply the same rule in all situations like the new physician. Overall, the point is that RSI is so powerful that it can be traded in both ways, that is, RSI can be traded on the basis of being overbought and oversold and trades can also be traded on the basis of RSI reversal.

If you are a new trader then do not panic. I am going to explain both types of trading by giving you practical examples.

I conducted a poll among my followers on YouTube to make a video on RSI, in which I asked them that if I want to show my new research by back testing it on one stock, which stock would they choose?

Now, my followers were smart because 51per cent of the followers asked me to back test HDFC Bank out of Reliance, TCS, HDFC Bank and Bharti Airtel (the four companies with the highest market cap).

Because during that period, on 2nd January, 2023, the price of HDFC Bank's share was ₹ 1,628.70 and even after almost one and a half years, the share, on 31st July, 2024, was trading at ₹ 1,615.75.

That is, if a person had held HDFC Bank for about one and a half years from 2nd January, 2023 to 31st July, 2024, then despite being a blue chip share, its return would have been in minus (1,628.70 to 1,615.75).

Therefore, my followers were smarter than me. They thought that any method can be successful in rising stocks, but it would be fun if I find a method to earn money in such stocks with negative returns and consolidating for almost one and a half years.

I accepted the above challenge of my followers and by back testing my trading setup based only on RSI, I showed them a profit of ₹ 23,842.69 in this stock without short selling.

Hence, in this chapter we will understand the same trade setup.

How to calculate RSI? Most traders never try to learn and understand the stock market in depth. They hear the name of any indicator, like the sennai decoction mentioned in this chapter, and then start trading on that basis.

Many of you readers who are not already my followers on YouTube may not know how RSI is calculated.

To understand any indicator in depth, one must know the basic principle of its calculation. So in today's chapter, I will first teach you how to calculate RSI, which is very simple.

Look carefully at the data in the picture given below –

In this picture, you are shown the data of HDFC Bank from 2nd January, 2023 to 30th January, 2023.

Now let us learn to calculate RSI based on this data.

1. First of all, after downloading the data, add two columns – first for profit, second for loss.
2. If the stock has closed higher than the previous day, then in the profit column, write the number of rupees by which the stock closed higher; but if the stock closed lower, then instead of writing minus in the profit column, write only 'zero'.

   For example, on 2nd January, 2023, the close price of the stock was 1,628.70 and on 3rd January, the close price of the stock was 1,639.35, so in the profit column, after subtracting 1,628.70 from 1,639.35, the stock has increased by rupees 10.65, so 10.65 is written.

   But on 4th January, the stock fell by rupees 29.30, so in the profit column, instead of writing a figure in the minus, only 'zero' is written.
3. Similarly, if the stock closes with a fall, then whatever decline is there, it should be written in the loss column without a minus sign that there is a fall of so many rupees; but when the stock closes with a rise, then 'zero' should be written in the fall column. For example, if the stock closed at a gain of ₹ 10.65 on 3rd January as compared to 2nd January, then only 'zero' is written in the fall loss column and if the stock closed at a loss of ₹ 29.30 on 4th January, 2023, then 'zero' is written in the profit column and 29.30 in the loss column.

HDFC Bank Price Data from 2nd January, 2023 to 30th January, 2023

Month	Open	High	Low	Close	Profit	Loss	Average profit in last 14 days	Average loss in last 14 days	RS	RSI
02 January, 2023	1,627.00	1,639.75	1,618.55	1,628.70						
03 January, 2023	1,622.20	1,643.00	1,622.20	1,639.35	10.65	0				
04 January, 2023	1,635.00	1,645.75	1,607.00	1,610.05	0	29.3				
05 January, 2023	1,615.00	1,618.05	1,589.40	1,599.70	0	10.35				
06 January, 2023	1,602.00	1,609.10	1,578.20	1,594.40	0	5.3				
09 January, 2023	1,596.00	1,611.55	1,590.00	1,597.50	3.1	0				
10 January, 2023	1,600.00	1,600.00	1,565.00	1,568.30	0	29.2				
11 January, 2023	1,567.95	1,598.00	1,560.00	1,590.90	22.6	0				
12 January, 2023	1,587.80	1,603.90	1,584.15	1,599.40	8.5	0				
13 January, 2023	1,598.75	1,609.90	1,586.00	1,600.65	1.25	0				
16 January, 2023	1,615.00	1,621.30	1,580.30	1,585.30	0	15.35				
17 January, 2023	1,589.80	1,611.00	1,577.50	1,608.90	23.6	0				
18 January, 2023	1,605.00	1,641.60	1,599.70	1,637.30	28.4	0				
19 January, 2023	1,637.00	1,650.00	1,633.00	1,644.10	6.8	0				
20 January, 2023	1,644.10	1,669.00	1,643.40	1,660.95	16.85	0	8.70	6.39	1.36	57.63
23 January, 2023	1,666.25	1,682.60	1,661.40	1,673.10	12.15	0	8.94	5.94	1.51	60.10
24 January, 2023	1,675.05	1,702.40	1,675.00	1,695.50	22.4	0	9.90	5.51	1.80	64.24
25 January, 2023	1,691.40	1,692.95	1,645.30	1,648.65	0	46.85	9.20	8.46	1.09	52.07
27 January, 2023	1,632.00	1,637.00	1,589.95	1,615.80	0	32.85	8.54	10.21	0.84	45.55
30 January, 2023	1,595.00	1,625.30	1,582.00	1,614.15	0	1.65	7.93	9.60	0.83	45.25

Now try to understand by looking at column F and G in the picture above, how when the stock rises from the previous day, that much is written in the profit column, then 'zero' comes in loss and the amount by which the stock falls in the previous day, that much is written in the loss column, then 'zero' comes in the profit column.

4. Now in column H and I, we calculate the average profit and loss of 14 days. Hence, these columns have been kept blank for the first 14 days, because to start calculating the average requires at least 14 days of data.

5. Now divide the 14 days average profit, i.e., data in column H by the 14 days average loss, i.e., data in column I. This is called Relative Strength, i.e., RS.

   RS = 14 days average gain ÷ 14 days average loss

   Now you can understand in the above diagram that how the 14 days average gain was 8.70. On dividing it by the 14 days average loss, i.e., 6.39, 1.36 has come in the RS column.

6. Now J. Wells Wilder, the inventor of RSI, wanted to organise it like an index between 0 to 100, so he created a formula—

   RSI = 100 – (100 + RS).

   This gives the value of RSI between 0-100. As you can see in the above figure, when we plugged RS = 1.36 in this formula, we got RSI = 57.63.

7. Once the 14-day RSI is calculated, to calculate the average gains and average losses, we use 'exponential average' instead of simple average, in which the last day of the 14 days is given more weightage.

   I hope you understood the essence of RSI from the above examples. Now understand some general rules related to RSI. Then I will show you its application on the data of HDFC Bank for a period of 1.5 years in which the stock neither fell nor rose.

General rules related to RSI—

1. If RSI is above 70, then it is considered that the stock has entered the overbought zone and has become overvalued.
2. If RSI is below 30, then it is considered that the stock has entered the oversold zone and has become undervalued.
3. Therefore, if RSI is above 70, then the general rule is to book profits and if RSI is below 30, then the general rule is to make fresh purchases.
4. Here we are talking about making this purchase for holding in the cash market, because RSI is calculated on the basis of 14 days average. Therefore, if you make purchases on the basis of RSI, then you should have a view to hold at least for 14 days to 90 days.
5. Nowadays, the form of RSI has been distorted a lot. People ask you to trade by applying it on intraday charts, one- hour charts, 5-minute charts and keep a strict stop loss in it. In this type of trade, when the stop loss gets triggered, most of the novices and hasty traders lose money and start blaming the stock market.

Please remember my motto that 'gambling is not for anyone', so do not treat the stock market like gambling but like investment and business.

The five rules that I have told you above are general rules related to RSI. But in the present times, you will also get to hear some such principles that –

1. When the RSI of a stock goes above 70, at the same time it comes into strong momentum. Now this means that the stock whose RSI is above 70 has closed with gains on most of the days in the last 14 days. So, it is not wise to sell such a stock with strong momentum. Therefore, some experts of this type call RSI going above 70 as 'trade reversal' and advise to buy on such trade reversal.
2. Similarly, when RSI goes below 30, then 'bear trade reversal' takes place and they advise to sell in such stock.

Now the two rules of trade reversal mentioned above are completely opposite to the basic rules of RSI. Buyers in this type of trade reversal often get trapped at very high levels and those who short when RSI goes below 30 also suffer huge losses due to the stock rising rapidly.

Actually, the above trade reversal tips are for very short- term swing traders or intraday or option traders, who have to be satisfied with 1-2 per cent profit due to strong momentum and also have to keep very strict stop loss.

In the HDFC Bank example mentioned above, in a period of 1.5 years, this type of RSI crossed 70 four times, in which twice you got a target of 3.14 per cent, but twice this type of breakout proved wrong and after the strong RSI went above 70, it came back down without touching the target.

Now, since my methods do not have a stop loss, after a long research, I have made some rules to buy stocks based on RSI and exit with a profit of at least 6.28 per cent.

Thus, with the rules made by me, if you trade in blue chip stocks, you can easily get a target of up to 6.28 per cent without placing a stop loss.

Using these rules, I showed my followers that I booked a profit of ₹ 23,842 in HDFC Bank even in the consolidated period when the stock did not move at all in 1.5 years, which was surprising for my followers. Readers who are interested in seeing the full results of this research can search for the video titled 'Complete System of Swing Trading using only RSI on my channel.

In the next chapter, I will explain to you the description of these rules and the complete method of trading in the blue chip stocks of Nifty 50 and Nifty Next 50 based on these rules.

❑

10

Nifty's Shop

In 2013, I wrote my first book on the stock market in English titled 'The Winning Theory in Stock Market'. At that time, this book was published from the USA. Later, when I gave the rights of publishing it in India to 'Prabhat Prakashan', they published this book under the new name, 'How to Make Profit in Share Market', whose Hindi version is titled '*Share Bazar Me Safal Kaise Hon*?'.

In the first chapter of this book, I suggested to you to work in the stock market from the 'shopkeeper's point of view'.

For those who have not read the said book, let me describe the shopkeeper's point of view once again, so that it becomes a little easier for you to understand why I have used the name 'Nifty's Shop' in this chapter.

A shopkeeper understands doing business very well. Go to your nearest grocery shop. There you will find many items like incense sticks, soap, shampoo, razor, pulses, rice, cheese, biscuits, Chyavanaprash, toothpaste etc.

Now whatever item a customer comes to the shop for, the shopkeeper sells it to him by making a profit of about 6-7 per cent due to the wide variety of items available in the shop. For example, a customer comes and asks, "Do you have dates?" So since it is a big grocery store, he gets dates. Another customer comes and asks, "Do you have coconut?" The shopkeeper sells coconut to him as well.

Thus, by selling goods at a margin of 6-7per cent, the shopkeeper earns so much that he can manage a better lifestyle even after paying shop rent, transport expenses, electricity bill, wages, servant expenses and other expenses.

But diversified portfolio is not maintained in these shares; hence, different shares of different sectors are not managed in the market every day.

The shopkeeper keeps rotating money at a profit of 6-7per cent and is able to generate strong returns on his capital by rotation of money. But the small investor, unaware of this art, keeps holding in the greed of big profits and is deprived of the benefits of rotation of money.

The shopkeeper does not keep a stop loss. Suppose, a shopkeeper has a soap worth rupees 20 and he himself has bought it for rupees 16, but the customer is ready to pay only rupees 14 for the soap, then will the shopkeeper consider a stop loss of rupees 14 and sell the soap bought for 16 for 14 and book a loss of 2?

No, because the shopkeeper knows that as long as my goods (my soap) are with me, I can incur a loss on it only when I sell it at a lower price. But if not today, then tomorrow, a customer who will pay rupees 20 for that soap will also come to the market. The most important thing is that if the shopkeeper's goods are kept in the shop for a long time without being sold, then it can get spoiled, but if our shares are of blue chip companies, then instead of getting spoiled, they give us dividends during the holding period.

So, keeping in mind the shopkeeper's perspective, I have created a method of earning regular income by buying blue chip stocks of Nifty 50 and Nifty Next 50 on the basis of RSI, rotating my money by taking a profit of 6.28 per cent, which I have named 'Nifty's Shop'. This method got a lot of appreciation from India and abroad and by the time I wrote the book, it had more than 6 lakh views on YouTube.

In today's chapter, I am going to explain this method to you.

The main rules of trading with this method based on RSI are as follows -

1. In 'Nifty's Shop', trade only in the blue chip stocks of Nifty 50 and Nifty Next 50.

2. You have to consider buying those stocks among Nifty 50 and Nifty Next 50 whose RSI has gone below 35; but do not buy all those stocks together, because in a day there can be more than one stock whose RSI has gone below 35. Therefore, the rules of how to buy them will be told to you later.

3. If you do not want to search for stocks with RSI less than 35 manually, then you can create a Google Finance Sheet for it, which gets updated automatically by Google. It tells that now the RSI of this stock has gone below 35, so we have to start buying. You can learn this type of Google Finance Sheet by watching the related video on my YouTube channel, or by searching my blog named 'Share Genius', you can copy this sheet with a new name and save it in your Google Drive from the link given in the back test of this method.

4. If you are using Google Finance Sheet, then we take the RSI after the market closes. Google Sheet gets updated late, so before placing an order, check whether today's date has been updated in Google Sheet. Often, it gets updated after 12 o'clock at night, so the best time to place an order is 6 am to 9 am before the market opens.

5. The shares whose RSI is less than 35 are bought by placing an order for the next day through aftermarket order at its close price.

6. If RSI of more than one share is less than 35, then the one with the lowest is bought first. In this, only one share has to be bought in a day, not more than that. So, remember that if RSI of more than one share is less than 35, then the one with the lowest RSI is bought first.

7. The share with low RSI is in bear phase and there is no guarantee that it will not fall further. So, in this method, instead of buying at one time, an attempt is made to minimise the average price by buying up to 7 times when RSI is less than 35, 30, 25, 20, 15, 10, 5. If there is a bounce back anywhere in between and you get a profit above 6.28 per cent on the average price, then you have to exit.

8. A profit of 6.28 per cent is not less. I have determined this after a long research, which I will explain to you in a new chapter titled 'My Research on the Physics of Share Market' or you will find its complete research in my upcoming ninth book. For now, understand that the value of π in physics is approximately 3.14. The value of π has a surprising use in the rules of Ishwar, Allah, God, Wahe Guru, which govern the entire universe. Before my long research, I used to think it to be 2.75 per cent and I thought that the figure of 2.75 per cent fits most of the research accurately. Then I found that this 3 per cent is more correct. At that time I thought 2 π is 6 per cent, but then I found that the value of π is actually 3.14, and for profit booking, the figure above 2 π, i.e., 6.28 per cent, is the best.

9. Divide your capital into 50 equal parts and invest only one part at a time and in a day. The stock market is always risky, so there is no guarantee that these 50 will never fall short. But I have found that generally in the normal market, if the capital is divided into 50 parts and invested only one part at a time, then due to profit booking and rotation of the amount, usually 50 parts do not fall short. But if there is a very bear market and 50 parts fall short, then we can add some more amount as per our capacity or we can wait for profit booking to make new purchases.

10. Do not hurry in averaging. If you buy a stock with RSI below 35 and it closes below 30, then before buying it for averaging, two things have to be checked:

    (a) Firstly, if there is any other new stock worth buying in the sheet that day, then buy that first. That is, we try to keep the shop as diversified as possible. If no other new stock is in the range of buying, then consider other stocks. In that, first you have to see the RSI levels. If you make a purchase below the level of 35, then for averaging, the purchase should be at least below the level of 30. If you have averaged below the level of 30, then the next average should be below the level of 25.

(b) The second thing to check is that at the time of purchase for averaging, the market price of your stock should have fallen by at least 3.14 per cent from your last purchase price. Now suppose there are 3 stocks which are suitable for averaging. RSI of one has gone below 20, of another has gone below 25, and of the third has gone below 30, then you have to see which of the three stocks has fallen the most from its last purchase? Suppose, one stock has fallen by only 2.80 per cent from its last purchase, but its RSI is below 20; the second has fallen by 3.15 per cent, its RSI is below the level of 25; and the third one has fallen by 10 per cent and its RSI is below 30. First buy the one that has fallen by the maximum 10 per cent, and for the rest, we will decide after checking the sheet again the next day. Remember here that the fall in percentage is not to be taken from the average price but from the last purchase.

11. If at any stage, your share falls more than 20 per cent from your average price, then understand that it has entered the long- term bear phase. Hence, it has to be taken out of the system and in order to save the principal amount invested in it and also to exit with a profit of 6.28 per cent, one has to buy it once a month with 1/15th of the amount invested in it like a SIP every month and average it till it gets a profit of more than 6 per cent. For example, if you had invested ₹ 15,000 in a stock and that stock goes out of the index for some reason and falls by more than 20 per cent, then instead of panicking, you should buy 1/15 of 15,000, i.e., ₹ 1,000 per month, or if the price of the stock is more than 1,000, then at least one share per month should be bought for averaging until you get a profit of

6.28 per cent from the average price. According to my research, if your company does not close down the business and get delisted, then usually, you can exit in this way in blue chip companies. The stock market is risky. Before averaging in this way, you should always keep in mind your risk- taking capacity.

12. Now if you feel that you are not able to understand these rules, then do not worry. For you, I have given the practical real back test of at least three months of this method on my 'Share Genius' blog. If you read the 3 months data of my daily buying and selling, then you will understand everything. You can read it on the above mentioned 'Share Genius' blog or by searching 'Nifty Ki Dukan: Mahesh Kaushik's Real Back Test'.

❑

11

Buying on Breakout of Weekly Highs

If a new investor says to me, "Sir, you have told many methods of the stock market and I am not able to decide which of these methods should I start with" then I always advise him to start with 'Darvas Box Theory'.

On 29th July, 2019, I first published a video on my channel, whose name was - 'You will forget the technical chart, when you will understand this Darvas Box trading indicator'. Since then, I still get emails from my lakhs of followers spread across the country and abroad that they are trading only with Darvas Box Theory. That is, for five years from 2019 to 2024, many of my followers are earning good profit by trading only with Darvas Box Theory.

To understand the Darvas Box Theory, first understand the story of Nicholas Darvas.

Nicholas Darvas was born in 1920. He was a dancer by profession. He and his half-sister toured Europe and the United States, performing in dance shows. Once a drama company offered him shares in exchange for his dance fees. From there, his interest in the stock market was aroused.

Initially, he used to buy shares based on the advice of his broker and rumours going on in the market, due to which he had to suffer heavy losses many times. Then he read Gerald M. Loeb's book, 'The Battle for Investment Survival', published in 1935 and Humphrey Bancroft

Neill's book ,'Tape Reading and Market Tactics', published in 1931. This aroused his interest in studying and developing his own theory.

That is why you should also keep reading books on the stock market as I do myself, because who knows, the world may get its next Nicolas Darvas from among you.

Anyway, he was a dancer and without paying attention to the advice of his brokers as well as rumours and news, he created a trading system with his own mind. That is called the 'Darvas Box Theory'. He used to draw a box with his hand on the stock chart, as you can see in the picture below—

Darvas Box

He would buy when the stock price moved from one box to another. You can also think of it as a type of Pivot Point Breakout on the chart.

But for you retail investors, it is a bit difficult to understand this type of Darvas Box indicator or to buy from a system based on Pivot Point Breakout. So I simplified this system to 'buy on breakout above the weekly high', which is much simpler and more accurate.

Nicolas Darvas made $24,50,000 from this system in 18 months during the bull market of 1957-1958, which is approximately $1.8 billion today.

So let us start learning this method.

The picture below shows the data of Yes Bank from August 10, 2018 to August 16, 2018.

Yes Bank Data for Darvas Box

Symbol	Date Price	Open price	High price	Low price	Close price	
Yes Bank	10th August 2018	382	391	381	382.85	Box 391-368
Yes Bank	13th August 2018	379	383	368.3	370.7	
Yes Bank	14th August 2018	369	384.3	368.15	382.5	
Yes Bank	16th August 2018	381.2	384.85	374.2	378.45	

Here, 10th August, 2018 was Friday and 16th August, 2018 was Thursday, which means that the data for the expiry week from Friday to Thursday is shown here.

If we make a Darvas box based on this data, then the highest level of the box is 391 and the lowest level is 368. This means that whatever high is formed this week, it has to be rounded up a little above that. Here the high is 391, which is already rounded up. Whatever low is formed has to be rounded down a little below that. Here the lowest level was 368.15, so it has to be rounded down a little to 368.

So this week's Darvas box is between 391-368. Now Nicholas Darvas believed that as long as the stock keeps trading in the middle of this box, it should neither be bought nor sold; but if the range of the box is broken, that is, if it crosses the highest level in the next week's trade, then the stock will rise and can be bought. Here it is also said for traders that if it goes away from the lowest level of the box, that is, 368, then it is a bearish signal and short selling can be done in the stock. Although this is true to a large extent, remember, Nicholas Darvas himself never did short selling or intraday in his life. Whatever he earned, he earned it by buying shares for swing trading and holding them.

So, to maintain the original form of Nicholas Darvas' method, I will also not advise you to go for short selling.

So, overall, the bottom line is that next week if the stock crosses a little above the previous week's high, i.e., ₹ 391, then we can buy it for a swing trading target of 3.14 per cent.

Here the target of 3.14 per cent is equal to the value of π. In the following chapters, you will find a chapter named 'My Research on the Physics of Stock Market'. There we will discuss how the target of 1 π = 3.14 per cent is most likely to come for swing trading.

Now see the data of next week in the following figure.

Data for next week's Darvas Box

Symbol	Date price	Open price	High price	Low price	Close price	
Yes Bank	17th August 2018	382.40	395.65	380.3	393.2	Box 404-380
Yes Bank	20th August 2018	396.8	404	392.55	394	
Yes Bank	21st August 2018	396	397.45	389.5	391.35	
Yes Bank	23rd August 2018	395.25	395.5	383.35	388.6	

You can see that next week, on 17th August, you could have easily bought Yes Bank shares at a price of ₹ 391. Nowadays brokers allow you to fill GTT (Good Till Trigger) orders, meaning you can place an order for 391 in advance. During the week, whenever the stock moved above 391, the stock would have been bought for you and the target of 3.14 per cent of 391 was 403.27. You can see that on 20th August, the stock made a high of 404, meaning you would have achieved this target in 3 days of holding.

Darvas Box Theory is also used for such short- term trading or for holding with a little patience, where you can keep a target of 6.28 per cent (equivalent to 2 π). Some people also consider it right to keep a target of 1.5 π, that is 4.71 per cent.

But in such a situation, when the target is 4.71 per cent or 6.28 per cent and the stock gets triggered by touching the highest level of the previous week, but after that, it starts falling back without giving the target, then the next time whenever the highest level of the box is triggered, one will have to buy back for averaging. In this, we have to keep in mind that for new purchase, the difference in price should be at least 3.14 per cent more than the previous purchase, otherwise many times, a lot of your money gets stuck by buying at small intervals.

What I mean to say is that if you bought at 404, then the next purchase should be either above 416.68 or below 391.31.

Well, now if you place a buy order for the next week at the highest level of the box at 404, then your order will not get triggered because the stock did not trigger its previous week's highest level in any week after that till 4th October, 2018.

You can see this data together in the following figure—

In the above figure, you saw that your box was 223-165 for the week ending on 4th October, 2018. In other words, if you had placed an order to trigger above 223, the stock would have triggered above 223 on 8th October and then gone up to 268.95. See the following figure—

Different targets in a single week

Symbol	Date price	Open price	High price	Low price	Close price	
Yes Bank	5th October 2018	215	218.50	203.1	206	
Yes Bank	8th October 2018	210	226.6	207.4	221.2	
Yes Bank	9th October 2018	225.5	233.8	222.6	224.65	Box 269-203
Yes Bank	10th October 2018	229	237	219.4	233.9	
Yes Bank	11th October 2018	222	268.95	216.65	240.2	

In other words, you could have got targets of 3.14 per cent, 4.71 per cent or even above 6.28 per cent in the same week.

But this does not happen every time. Even if you do not get the target, you have to continue buying for averaging when the highest level is formed and I have told you the example of Yes Bank. This method is effective even in stocks with heavy fall. I have told this for the sake of explaining, otherwise you should use this method in good blue chip stocks and in such stocks, which have made their annual low level.

For the 'Darvas Box Theory', ideally, you should divide your fund into nine parts and trade. What I mean to say here is that if you want to trade in five shares using Darvas Box Theory and you have a fund of ₹ 2 lakh, then first divide 2 lakh by 5 and get a fund of ₹ 40,000 for one share. Now divide 40000 by 9 and an order of ₹ 4,444 will have to be placed in a week, so that if the order gets triggered and the share falls

No triggering for several weeks

Symbol	Date price	Open price	High price	Low price	Close price	
Yes Bank	24th August 2018	387	388.7	372.85	374.2	
Yes Bank	27th August 2018	378	384.65	377	383	Box 389-358
Yes Bank	28th August 2018	386	386	362.8	370.6	
Yes Bank	29th August 2018	373.65	378.55	362	365.15	
Yes Bank	30th August 2018	369	369	358	361.75	
Yes Bank	31st August 2018	343	350	336.35	343.5	
Yes Bank	3rd September 2018	347.95	348	337.2	339.05	Box 350-332
Yes Bank	4th September 2018	340.75	343.4	332.55	334.05	
Yes Bank	5th September 2018	332.9	344.9	332.35	343.8	
Yes Bank	6th September 2018	346.55	347.8	337.9	339.2	
Yes Bank	7th September 2018	341	341.05	321.8	323.4	Box 342-310
Yes Bank	10th September 2018	323.65	328.9	316	323.65	
Yes Bank	11th September 2018	326	327.85	314.6	316.6	
Yes Bank	12th September 2018	318	319.95	310.6	314.3	

Yes Bank	14th September 2018	318.5	328.5	316.7	323.1	
Yes Bank	17th September 2018	317.5	321.85	315.95	318.6	Box 329-315
Yes Bank	18th September 2018	319.35	328.95	319.1	323.55	
Yes Bank	19th September 2018	326	328.75	318.05	319.2	
Yes Bank	21st September 2018	287.3	287.3	218.1	226.5	
Yes Bank	24th September 2018	236.5	237.5	215.85	226.4	Box 288-197
Yes Bank	25th September 2018	230	238.85	197.25	219.7	
Yes Bank	26th September 2018	223	229.8	217	223.75	
Yes Bank	27th September 2018	226	227	202.05	203.25	
Yes Bank	28th September 2018	203.6	204	165	183.65	
Yes Bank	1st October 2018	180	203.8	170.6	200.85	Box 223-165
Yes Bank	3rd October 2018	205	222.95	202.25	212.75	
Yes Bank	4th October 2018	209.4	220	205.05	215	

back and you have to buy again in the coming weeks, then even after buying nine times, your fund will not fall short and by then, the target will be achieved. The tarWget has to be calculated on the average price.

Now for this method, what is the easiest way to select such stocks which have already made their annual low level? To select such stocks, you can create your own Google Finance Sheet which gets automatically updated from Google Finance. So let us understand the method of creating this sheet and the formulae used in it. If you create this sheet, it will get automatically updated from Google Finance and whether the market is up or down, you can create this Google Finance Sheet and select the best stocks for swing trading using the 'Darvas Box Theory'.

To create such a sheet, use only a desktop or laptop, because typing the sheet's formulae on mobile is difficult. Once you have created the sheet, if you want, you can open and view it on mobile by downloading the 'Google Sheets' app. But in the beginning, you should use a desktop or laptop to create a sheet.

We will learn to create it step-by-step. First of all, open Google Drive. If you are facing difficulty in understanding the steps written here, then I have made a video on YouTube and explained all the steps. You can watch this video from the following link -

https://www.youtube.com/watch?v = b0sofgWSPdw

If you face difficulty in searching the video from this link, then this is a video of class 3 of my 'Mahesh Kaushik Ki Pathshala' series, which you can watch by searching directly.

Go to your Google Drive and click on New and then click on Google Sheets. This will open a new Google Sheet named Untitled Spreadsheet.

You can change its name by clicking on Untitled Spreadsheet in this sheet. You can give any name as per your wish, like here I am giving the name, Best Stocks for Darvas BoÛ Theory Swing Trading.

Now title the first row of the sheet REIT and INVIT. In this, we will select those REIT and INVIT shares which are worth swing trading right now because swing trading in these shares using Darvas Box method gives additional profit on hold shares due to payment of rent and dividend every 4 months. Those who do not know what REIT INVIT are can gather more information about this by reading my book, 'How to attain financial freedom with the miracle of SIP'.

In the first column, enter the names of Reit Invit. We will select only seven major stocks appearing in NIfty Riet Invit Index and write their names in the first column and their BSE Code in the second column.

BSE code is written because Google Finance does not yet capture Reit Invit from the data of NSE Code. So, in this, we will need BSE Code for Reit Invit.

The formulae used in the sheet are as follows—

Formula for CMP = GOOGLEFINANCE(B3,"price")

52- Week High = GOOGLEFINANCE(B3,"high52")52

52- week high date: = to_date(index(sort(GOOGLEFINANC

E(B3, "high", today()-52*7, today(), "DAILY"),2,0),2,1)

52- week Low = GOOGLEFINANCE(B3,"low52")

52- Week Low Date = to_date(index(sort(GOOGLEFINANC

E(B3, "low", today()-52*7, today(), "DAILY"),2,1),1,1))

Output = if(AND(G3>E3),"Stock in green zone","Stock in

red zone")

Then go to the Format Menu of the sheet and select Conditional

Formatting. In that, in the range H3:H9, select Format Cell if :- Text Contains. Write green in the box, then select green colour in the colour and click Done. This will highlight the cells containing the word 'green' in green colour.

Similarly, go to the Format Menu of the sheet and select Conditional Formatting.

Select Format Cell if:-Text Contains from the range H3:H9, write red in the box, then select red colour and click Done. This will highlight the cells with the word 'red' in red.

A plus sign is given below. Add a new sheet with it and fill in the NSE codes of the 250 stocks of Nifty Large Mid Cap 250 Index and copy and paste all the formulae from the previous sheet. Keep in mind here that A3 has to be used in place of B3, because there is no B column with BSE code here.

For more information, you can see the formulae in my sheet shown in the video.

Now select all the columns in the sheet, go to Data Menu, select Short Range, then go to Advanced Shorting Option and short column C. This will bring those stocks at the top which made 52- week high a long time ago, meaning, they have been consolidated for a long time. Therefore, trade them on priority basis first.

Now those readers who are not very good at making Google Sheets and are facing problems, they can watch the video of class 3 of 'Mahesh Kaushik Ki Pathshala' series on my YouTube channel. In that, I have described how to make such a sheet in the video.

Still, if you are facing problems, a link to such a sheet made by me has been given in the description of the video. You can open it and use it or you can open the sheet made by me from the description of the video and copy it with a new name in your Google Drive. If you are facing any problem with the above formula, then read the comments below the video. You mess up the formula by adding extra spaces etc. many such comments have been answered.

Apart from that, it is very easy to select stocks for Darvas Box Theory. If the date on which you are trading has a yearly low in the months preceding that date, then understand that the stock is moving up after making its yearly low and if it is falling from its yearly high in the months just preceding your trade date, then let it bottom out.

Many of my followers are getting good results by investing in the stocks selected in the Super Breakout and Consolidated Breakout method mentioned in this book using the Darvas Box Theory.

❑

12

How can ₹ 2 lakh Become ₹ 20 crores through the Power of Compounding?

The story of Sumpadu told by me about compounding is very famous. If you have not heard it, then I will tell you the story first in the book; then based on the teachings of the story, we will learn to do compounding in the stock market.

A businessman named Sumpadu lived in a town called Malgudi. That businessman had 10 sons, all of whom were useless and did not do any work. Sumpadu was getting old day by day. He had a blanket shop in the town. By selling blankets all his life, he had collected a capital of rupees 2 lakh with great difficulty.

Now one day, Sumpadu called his ten sons and told them, *"I have become very old and I want to give one crores rupees to each of you children"*.

The sons thought that their father had lost his mind because they knew very well that their father had barely rupees 2-3 lakh. Then how could he get rupees 10 crores to give them?

Still, Sumpadu explained to them that what is the harm in trying? He said that he would give each of them blankets worth rupees 15 thousand to sell. They had to go to the nearest village and sell each blanket, earning a profit of 6.28 per cent on it.

He said, *"Not only this, I will also pay you the fare for travelling from this town to the nearest village and expenses for food and drink, and whatever profit amount remains after deducting expenses and tax, I will take half of it for household expenses and the remaining half amount I will add to the original amount of ₹ 20,000 each time to give you more blankets worth that much to sell. If you sell blankets in this way only 31 times, then your original amount will be doubled, that too after deducting all expenses"*.

After this, Sumpadu started explaining to them the calculation of deducting expenses, deducting income tax and keeping half the amount for household expenses.

I am showing you this calculation in the form of a table. In this, I have taken brokerage and charges instead of travel expenses, because we do not have to travel from one village to another to sell shares. Our expenses are in the form of brokerage, STT and DP charges. In this calculation, I have added brokerage on both sides of buying and selling as per my broker and rupees 16 DP charge. You can calculate by increasing or decreasing as per your broker and preparing your own excel sheet.

In this, I have added short term capital gain tax of 20 per cent on profit as income tax; after that, I have added education cess of 4 per cent on tax; and after all this, I have made a provision to keep half of the profit remaining as self-dividend and the remaining half is to be added in the next trade as growth amount.

As shown in this picture, the calculation of the first 31 statuses is shown-

You can understand that if the first investment was of ₹ 15,000, then after earning a profit of 6.28 per cent and doing 31 trades, the principal amount became ₹ 30,182.64. Along with this, you also earned a self-dividend of ₹ 15,897.33, which means that with this type of compounding, your amount doubled in 31 trades and you got your principal amount back in the form of self-dividend. Apart from the ₹ 15,000 that was your initial investment, you get a self-dividend of 6.28

Compounding in 31 Phases

Step	Investment	After 6.28% Profit Valve	Profit Amountt	Brokerage Plus Charges Both Side	Remain Profit	Income Tax	Profit after Tax	Self Dividend For home expences	Growth Amount after Tax and Dividend
1	15000.00	15942.00	942.00	53.13	888.87	184.88	703.98	351.99	351.99
2	15351.99	16316.10	964.11	54.00	910.10	189.30	720.80	360.40	360.40
3	15712.39	16699.13	986.74	54.89	931.84	193.82	738.02	369.01	369.01
4	16081.40	17091.32	1009.91	55.81	954.10	198.45	755.65	377.83	377.83
5	16459.23	17492.87	1033.64	56.74	976.90	203.19	773.70	386.85	386.85
6	16846.08	17904.01	1057.93	57.70	1000.23	208.05	792.19	396.09	396.09
7	17242.17	18324.98	1082.81	58.68	1024.13	213.02	811.11	405.55	405.55
8	17647.73	18756.01	1108.28	59.68	1048.59	218.11	830.49	415.24	415.24
9	18062.97	19197.33	1134.35	60.71	1073.64	223.32	850.32	425.16	425.16
10	18488.13	19649.19	1161.05	61.76	1099.29	228.65	870.64	435.32	435.32
11	18923.45	20111.84	1188.39	62.84	1125.55	234.11	891.44	445.72	445.72
12	19369.17	20585.55	1216.38	63.95	1152.44	239.71	912.73	456.37	456.37
13	19825.54	21070.58	1245.04	65.08	1179.97	245.43	934.53	467.27	467.27
14	20292.80	21567.19	1274.39	66.23	1208.16	251.30	956.86	478.43	478.43
15	20771.23	22075.67	1304.43	67.42	1237.02	257.30	979.72	489.86	489.86
16	21261.09	22596.29	1335.20	68.63	1266.57	263.45	1003.12	501.56	501.56
17	21762.65	23129.35	1366.69	69.87	1296.82	269.74	1027.08	513.54	513.54
18	22276.19	23675.14	1398.94	71.14	1327.80	276.18	1051.62	525.81	525.81

Step	Investment	After 6.28% Profit Valve	Profit Amountt	Brokerage Plus Charges Both Side	Remain Profit	Income Tax	Profit after Tax	Self Dividend For home expences	Growth Amount after Tax and Dividend
19	22802.00	24233.97	1431.97	72.44	1359.52	282.78	1076.74	538.37	538.37
21	23340.38	24806.15	1465.78	73.78	1392.00	289.54	1102.46	551.23	551.23
21	23891.61	25392.00	1500.39	75.14	1425.25	296.45	1128.80	564.40	564.40
22	24456.01	25991.84	1535.84	76.54	1459.30	303.53	1155.77	577.88	577.88
23	25033.89	26606.02	1572.13	77.97	1494.16	310.79	1183.38	591.69	591.69
24	25625.58	27234.86	1609.29	79.43	1529.85	318.21	1211.64	605.82	605.82
25	26231.40	27878.73	1647.33	80.93	1566.40	325.81	1240.59	620.29	620.29
26	26851.69	28537.98	1686.29	82.47	1603.82	333.59	1270.22	635.11	635.11
27	27486.81	29212.98	1726.17	84.04	1642.13	341.56	1300.57	650.28	650.28
28	28137.09	29904.10	1767.01	85.65	1681.36	349.72	1331.64	665.82	665.82
29	28802.91	30611.73	1808.82	87.30	1721.53	358.08	1363.45	681.72	681.72
30	29484.63	31336.27	1851.63	88.99	1762.65	366.63	1396.02	698.01	698.01
31	30182.64	32078.11	1895.47	90.71	1804.76	375.39	1429.37	714.68	714.68
					Total Self Dividend			15897.33	

per cent above it in 31 trades. After that, whatever money you have invested in the market is your profit.

While Sumpadu was explaining this, one of his sons, whose name was Akdu, said, "But this did not make ₹ 1 crores, it just doubled".

Now Sumpadu said, "In this method, as you proceed further, you take lesser steps due to the power of compounding. For example, if you continue this method for 62 steps, then this time, your principal amount becomes more than double, i.e., 62,460.50. As seen in the following picture—

Now in those days, the amount of ₹ 1 lakh was a very big amount, so one of Sumpadu's sons said, "I want to see in how many steps this amount becomes more than ₹ 1 lakh!" So Sumpadu showed in the following diagram how after 93 steps, this initial capital of ₹ 15,000 will turn into ₹ 1, 29,562.92 and they will also be able to save more than ₹ 3,000 as self-dividend after each trade.

In this way, if these steps of compounding are continued, then in the 278th step the original capital becomes ₹ 1, 01, 94,116.99. Not only this, the total self- dividend of these 278 steps is also ₹ 1,04,22,633.40 i.e., Sumpadu had 10 sons, so each son had blankets worth more than ₹ 1 crores. So the worth of the total blankets became more than ₹ 10 crores. Also, in the whole process Sumpadu got dividend of more than ₹ 1 crores from each son for the household expenses. Due to this, the total self dividend also became more than ₹ 10 crores. Overall, Sumpadu converted his ₹ 2 lakh into ₹ 20 crores through compounding.

You will also find the excel sheet of the above calculation in the description of my video, 'How to earn 20 crores from 2 lakhs'.

Now, this question must be coming in your mind that Sumpadu had rupees 2 lakh, and he gave only rupees 15,000 to each son. This means that he gave only rupees 1.50 lakh to 10 sons, so what happened to the remaining rupees 50,000?

Actually, when a son could not sell a blanket even after trying for a long time, his blanket would get torn and become old, then Sumpadu

Compounding in 31-62 Steps

Step	Investment	After 6.28% Profit Valve	Profit Amount	Brokerage Plus Charges Both Side	Remain Profit	Income Tax	Profit after Tax	Self Dividend For home expences	Growth Amount after Tax and Dividend
31	30182.64	32078.11	1895.47	90.71	1804.76	375.39	1429.37	714.68	714.68
32	30897.33	32837.68	1940.35	92.48	1847.87	384.36	1463.51	731.76	731.76
33	31629.08	33615.39	1986.31	94.29	1892.01	393.54	1498.47	749.24	749.24
34	32378.32	34411.68	2033.36	96.15	1937.21	402.94	1534.27	767.14	767.14
35	33145.45	35226.99	2081.53	98.05	1983.49	412.57	1570.92	785.46	785.46
36	33930.92	36061.78	2130.86	99.99	2030.87	422.42	1608.45	804.22	804.22
37	34735.14	36916.51	2181.37	101.98	2079.38	432.51	1646.87	823.44	823.44
38	35558.58	37791.66	2233.08	104.02	2129.06	442.84	1686.21	843.11	843.11
39	36401.68	38687.71	2286.03	106.11	2179.92	453.42	1726.50	863.25	863.25
40	37264.93	39605.17	2340.24	108.24	2231.99	464.25	1767.74	883.87	883.87
41	38148.80	40544.55	2395.74	110.43	2285.31	475.35	1809.97	904.98	904.98
42	39053.79	41506.36	2452.58	112.67	2339.91	486.70	1853.21	926.60	926.60
43	39980.39	42491.16	2510.77	114.97	2395.80	498.33	1897.48	948.74	948.74
44	40929.13	43499.47	2570.35	117.31	2453.03	510.23	1942.80	971.40	971.40
45	41900.53	44531.88	2631.35	119.72	2511.63	522.42	1989.21	994.61	994.61
46	42895.13	45588.95	2693.81	122.18	2571.63	534.90	2036.73	1018.37	1018.37
47	43913.50	46671.27	2757.77	124.70	2633.07	547.68	2085.39	1042.69	1042.69

48	44956.20	47779.44	2823.25	127.28	2695.97	560.76	2135.21	1067.60	1067.60
49	46023.80	48914.09	2890.29	129.93	2760.37	574.16	2186.21	1093.11	1093.11
50	47116.90	50075.85	2958.94	132.63	2826.31	587.87	2238.44	1119.22	1119.22
51	48236.12	51265.35	3029.23	135.40	2893.83	601.92	2291.91	1145.96	1145.96
52	49382.08	52483.27	3101.19	138.24	2962.96	616.29	2346.66	1173.33	1173.33
53	50555.41	53730.29	3174.88	141.14	3033.74	631.02	2402.72	1201.36	1201.36
54	51756.77	55007.09	3250.33	144.12	3106.21	646.09	2460.12	1230.06	1230.06
55	52986.83	56314.40	3327.57	147.16	3180.41	661.53	2518.89	1259.44	1259.44
56	54246.27	57652.94	3406.67	150.28	3256.39	677.33	2579.06	1289.53	1289.53
57	55535.80	59023.45	3487.65	153.47	3334.18	693.51	2640.67	1320.33	1320.33
58	56856.13	60426.70	3570.57	156.74	3413.83	710.08	2703.75	1351.88	1351.88
59	58208.01	61863.47	3655.46	160.09	3495.38	727.04	2768.34	1384.17	1384.17
60	59592.18	63334.57	3742.39	163.51	3578.88	744.41	2834.47	1417.24	1417.24
61	61009.41	64840.80	3831.39	167.02	3664.37	762.19	2902.18	1451.09	1451.09
62	62460.50	66383.02	3922.52	170.61	3751.91	780.40	2971.51	1485.76	1485.76

Compounding in 62-93 Steps

Step	Investment	After 6.28% Profit Valve	Profit Amount	Brokerage Plus Charges Both Side	Remain Profit	Income Tax	Profit after Tax	Self Dividend For home expences	Growth Amount after Tax and Dividend
62	62460.50	66383.02	3922.52	170.61	3751.91	780.40	2971.51	1485.76	1485.76
63	63946.26	67962.08	4015.83	174.29	3841.54	799.04	3042.50	1521.25	1521.25
64	65467.51	69578.87	4111.36	178.06	3933.30	818.13	3115.18	1557.59	1557.59
65	67025.10	71234.27	4209.18	181.91	4027.26	837.67	3189.59	1594.80	1594.80
66	68619.89	72929.22	4309.33	185.86	4123.47	857.68	3265.79	1632.89	1632.89
67	70252.79	74664.66	4411.88	189.90	4221.97	878.17	3343.80	1671.90	1671.90
68	71924.69	76441.56	4516.87	194.04	4322.83	899.15	3423.68	1711.84	1711.84
69	73636.53	78260.90	4624.37	198.28	4426.10	920.63	3505.47	1752.73	1752.73
70	75389.26	80123.71	4734.45	202.62	4531.83	942.62	3589.21	1794.60	1794.60
71	77183.87	82031.02	4847.15	207.06	4640.09	965.14	3674.95	1837.48	1837.48
72	79021.34	83983.88	4962.54	211.61	4750.93	988.19	3762.74	1881.37	1881.37
73	80902.71	85983.40	5080.69	216.26	4864.43	1011.80	3852.63	1926.31	1926.31
74	82829.03	88030.69	5201.66	221.03	4980.63	1035.97	3944.66	1972.33	1972.33
75	84801.36	90126.88	5325.53	225.91	5099.61	1060.72	4038.89	2019.45	2019.45
76	86820.80	92273.15	5452.35	230.91	5221.43	1086.06	4135.38	2067.69	2067.69
77	88888.49	94470.69	5582.20	236.03	5346.17	1112.00	4234.16	2117.08	2117.08
78	91005.57	96720.72	5715.15	241.27	5473.88	1138.57	4335.31	2167.66	2167.66

79	93173.23	99024.51	5851.28	246.64	5604.64	1165.77	4438.88	2219.44	2219.44
80	95392.67	101383.33	5990.66	252.13	5738.53	1193.61	4544.91	2272.46	2272.46
81	97665.12	103798.49	6133.37	257.76	5875.61	1222.13	4653.49	2326.74	2326.74
82	99991.87	106271.36	6279.49	263.52	6015.97	1251.32	4764.65	2382.33	2382.33
83	102374.19	108803.29	6429.10	269.41	6159.69	1281.21	4878.47	2439.24	2439.24
84	104813.43	111395.71	6582.28	275.45	6306.83	1311.82	4995.01	2497.51	2497.51
85	107310.93	114050.06	6739.13	281.63	6457.49	1343.16	5114.33	2557.17	2557.17
86	109868.10	116767.82	6899.72	287.96	6611.75	1375.24	5236.51	2618.25	2618.25
87	112486.36	119550.50	7064.14	294.44	6769.70	1408.10	5361.60	2680.80	2680.80
88	115167.16	122399.65	7232.50	301.08	6931.42	1441.73	5489.68	2744.84	2744.84
89	117912.00	125316.87	7404.87	307.87	7097.00	1476.18	5620.82	2810.41	2810.41
90	120722.41	128303.78	7581.37	314.83	7266.54	1511.44	5755.10	2877.55	2877.55
91	123599.96	131362.03	7762.08	321.95	7440.12	1547.55	5892.58	2946.29	2946.29
92	126546.25	134493.35	7947.10	329.29	7617.86	1584.51	6033.34	3016.67	3016.67
93	129562.92	137699.47	8136.55	336.71	7799.84	1622.37	6177.47	3088.74	3088.74

would make it beautiful by getting it dry cleaned and adding *zari-gota*, due to which even that old blanket would get sold. That is why Sumpadu had saved an extra fund of rupees 50,000 with him for getting such blankets dry cleaned and applying zari-gota to them.

Now, let us understand this in the language of the share market. It is not necessary that you get a profit of more than 6.28 per cent in every trade. Sometimes your share can also fall.

However, in the RSI method, we have already made a provision for averaging out, so if profit is booked simultaneously after averaging out 3 times, then we assume that the 3 steps are completed simultaneously.

However, in those methods like Consolidated Dated Breakout and Super Breakout, where there is no provision of averaging out, if the share falls more than 20 per cent then you make a monthly SIP equal to $1/15^{th}$ of the original capital invested. New readers should note here that SIP does not mean SIP in mutual funds. SIP is also done in shares and most brokers provide automatic SIP facility of buying a fixed amount of shares every month.

For example, if a share was bought for ₹ 30,182.64 at the 31st step and it falls by more than 20 per cent, then purchase has to be done every month for an average of 1/15 of 30,182.64, i.e., ₹ 2,012.17, until the share exits after giving a profit of 6.28 per cent above the average price. In this, on the additional amount that we have invested (SIP) in addition to the original amount, we get a profit of 6.28 per cent and you can take the entire amount in self-dividend.

People also ask that since shares cannot be bought in decimals in India, then how can shares of the amount equal to the amount of the entire step be bought? In other words, if the amount of the step is 30,182.64, then how will shares of 30,182.64 be bought?

So the answer is that you have to buy shares in whole numbers and you have to buy so many shares that the investment is slightly above 30,182.64. You should not buy less than this.

For example, suppose the price of the share is 3,615.28, then dividing 30,182.64 by 3,615.28 gives 8.34. Hence we have to buy 9 shares, even if the investment is slightly more.

Now the question arises that suppose we have to buy for averaging, then 1/15th of its investment is 2,012.17. Now if only one share is worth 3,615.28, then how will you buy it? The answer is that then we will buy at least 1 share.

The next criticism of this method is that in this, 10 sons have to sell blankets 278 times, which means that to go from rupees 2 lakh to rupees 20 crores, $278 \times 10 = 2,780$ trades will have to be done and 6.28 per cent profit will not be booked every day. At most, 2-3 stocks will book profit in a month, and if there is a fall in the market, even this will not happen. In such a situation, if we assume an average of 2 profits per month, then it will take 1,390 months for 2,780 steps and if we divide it by 12, it will take 115.83 years. In this time, our *Ram Naam Satya* (the name of Rama is the truth) will happen (In Hinduism, after death, 'Ram Naam Satya' is recited along with the funeral procession).

But the above statement is completely wrong. In this method, this happens when we wait for profit booking and take a new position by adding growth amount only after profit booking is done.

In the practical form of this method, I started it in my SBI demat account (I have demat accounts in 3 broker companies, in which I use different methods).

I started the above method from May 2022 by investing ₹ 15,000 in one share in my SBI account. I kept a provision of an initial capital of ₹ 5 lakh instead of ₹ 2 lakh in it. I did this because I considered 10 imaginary sons (like the story of Sumpadu), S-1, S-2, S-3, S-4, S-5, S-6, S-7, S-8, S-9, S-10, and I bought one share of ₹ 15,000 per day and allotted it to one son as per consolidated breakout in this method.

When ₹ 1,50,000 was invested from S-1 to S-10, then without waiting for profit booking I started allocating shares of ₹ 15,351.99 to each son for the next line for the next stage. You can understand that the first 10 shares were bought for ₹ 15,000, after that 15,351.99 was invested in the next 10 shares. Now in between, profit booking started in some stocks, so the stocks in which profit was booked, I would colour them green in the excel sheet, so that it is remembered that profit has been booked in them.

Overall, to reduce the time, Sumpadu has faith in the ability of his sons to sell blankets and if the number comes in the line, even if the earlier blankets are not sold, he also allots different varieties of blankets of the next step to his sons.

Thus, I kept following the line. In some, profit booking happened first, in some later. I tried to invest at least one share in a trading day and kept writing it in the excel sheet line by line like this – first 1 to 10 shares @15,000, second 11 to 20 shares @15,531.99 per share, in the third step 21 to 30 shares @ rupees 15,712.39 per share. Now I had kept a capital of rupees 5 lakh, so my work did not stop even when I held about 30 shares. Just like when someone is born, his death is certain, similarly I thought that if not today then tomorrow, profit booking will keep happening in some of these, before or after. In this, if I can buy 1 share in one trading session, then for 2,780 steps, if I can take trades for 200 days in a year, then dividing 2,780 by 200 will take about 13.9 years, which is not bad.

However, in this method, there were many trading sessions in which I could not take trades due to being busy. In between, the market fell, so for many days I could not take trades as no new shares came in the consolidated breakout sheet.

In this, Bandhan Bank and Credit ACC fell by more than 20 per cent, so I had to do SIP of 1/15th part in them every month. Sometimes one has to stop the line further due to waiting for profit booking and lack of funds.

Thus, in 29 months from May 2022 to September 2024, I could actually take 247 trades. Out of this, 30 stocks were held at the time of writing the book and profit was booked in 217. Out of the 30 stocks, 2 stocks had an SIP of 1/15th as they fell by more than 20 per cent.

Overall, in this way, I am averaging 8.5 trades a month, which means 2,780 trades will take 327 months, i.e., 27.25 years.

However, time is uncertain in stocks and there is no guarantee that the time taken will be the same or less or more. But the amount of ₹ 5 lakh to ₹ 20 crores is also very big and it does not seem difficult to wait because along with this profit booking, half of the dividend is also being given to oneself to meet one's expenses.

Meaning, even if it takes 27 years, you can still take a self-dividend of ₹ 10 crores in these 27 years. (Companies give separate dividend,that is different and sometimes profit booking is also available above 6.28 per cent, up to 7-8-10-12 per cent, that is also additional income.) If your portfolio increases from ₹ 5 lakh to ₹ 10 crores in 27 years, then I think it is a decent return.

Some greedy followers say that they will not take self-dividend. Whatever profit they get, they will add all of it to the growth account, due to which this journey will be completed sooner instead of 27-28 years. But this is wrong and impractical. If you do not take self-dividend and the market falls badly, then whatever you have earned will be lost once again. You may panic and shut down the system.

The second most important thing is, if you buy a stock at the level of ₹ 15 lakh and it falls by 20 per cent, then to average it, 1/15th of 15 lakh i.e., rupees 1 lakh per month will be required. From where will you get that amount? But if you give yourself half self-dividend, then by the time you reach this level, you will have already given yourself self-dividend of more than ₹ 15 lakh, so you will be able to arrange for this amount.

The next point is that if the capital is less, then it is not necessary that you average from 1/15th part only. You can also average gradually from 1/30th, 1/45th part.

Some followers say that averaging is dangerous. What if the company shuts down? So first of all, use this system only in good blue chip companies, and then it is not necessary that you average. You can directly hold and wait. Or if you use this method with Darvas Box Theory, RSI etc. then buying happens automatically as per the rule for averaging.

The point is not to lure you into investing. This chapter is to make you understand the fact that 6.28 per cent profit is not less and the importance of compounding. You should invest according to your investment advisor's advice and your risk- taking capacity. Always remember, the stock market is risky, so keep adequate measures for risk management.

In the introduction of this book, I had told you that today's investor is an educated and intelligent investor. He knows the compounding principle of mathematics that if he invests rupees 20,000 in a trade and gets 6 per cent profit in that trade and the next time if he adds rupees 1,200 of this 6 per cent profit back to the principal amount and takes a trade of 21,200 and then again books 6 per cent profit, adds it back to the principal amount and takes a trade of 22,472 next time, then by doing this 108 times only, his rupees 20,000 will become rupees 1, 00, 000, 00. Those who do not believe it can check this calculation with an Excel sheet or calculator.

But this fact is theoretical. I have developed its practical form in the form of 'Sumpadu's story'.

This chapter has no connection with technical analysis like price action breakout etc. But the 6.28 per cent profit that I have repeatedly told you to book is not such a small profit. To show its power and to make you aware of the power of compounding, I have included this chapter in this book.

For those who do not understand this chapter of the book completely, there are 5 videos related to compounding of ₹ 2 lakh to ₹ 20 crores on my channel. If you watch them too, your concepts will become quite clear.

❑

13

Trading Based on Pivot Point

You must have realised that whatever methods of technical analysis or action breakout trading I have mentioned in this entire book, I have not supported their use in intraday trading.

This is so because, overall, I do not encourage intraday trading, because in intraday, new traders often make huge losses by taking more positions than their capacity. The second point is that the duration of intraday is very limited. It becomes very difficult to predict the movement of the stock with certainty for this limited period.

Due to all these reasons, intraday becomes like a gamble. You already know my motto in this context that 'Gambling is no one's cup of tea'. Still, just as it is written on cigarette packets that 'Smoking is injurious to health', people still smoke. Similarly, many retail traders are unable to give up their intraday addiction.

So that those intraday addicted traders who are buying my book do not get disappointed, I have included this chapter in this book for them.

Actually, here I will try to tell you the method of intraday trading with almost zero loss and without stop loss, which is mostly used by floor traders.

Now what are these floor traders? Floor traders are those traders who trade sitting in the stock exchange. You must have seen in the news and in the share market scenes in serials and films that many traders in the exchange keep trading continuously on the computer screen. These traders who trade sitting in the exchange are called 'floor traders', who trade with their own money. That is why in case of high fluctuations in the market, the emotions on their faces are shown in serials, news and films.

Now these floor traders mostly trade in intraday. This is their full time job and they trade with their own money. Many floor traders earn money from intraday trading every day and earn their livelihood.

So, I am going to share with you in this chapter the method used by successful floor traders.

According to me, either you should not trade intraday at all or if you want to trade intraday and do not want to incur heavy losses, then you can follow the strategy of some successful floor traders based on pivot point. However, the stock market is risky and the purpose of this chapter is not to encourage you to trade intraday. Always act according to your risk- taking capacity and the advice of an investment advisor.

After this disclaimer, let us start learning this almost zero loss method based on pivot point.

Pivot point is simply the average price of the previous day's close price and the intraday high and low.

Tata Motors Price Data

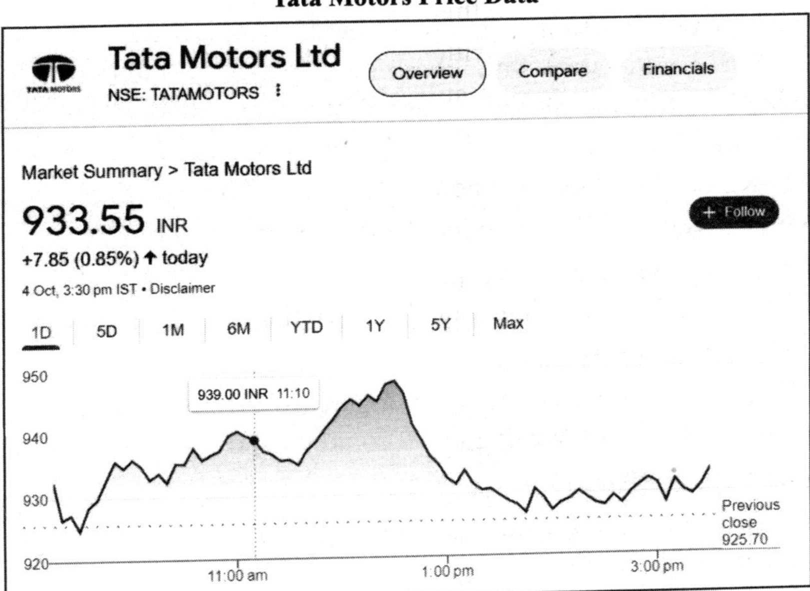

Understand it in practice from the chart of Tata Motors share dated 4th October, 2024.

The previous day close price of Tata Motors i.e., 3rd October, 2024, was 925.70, which is shown by the dotted line in the above chart.

At 11:10 am, its market price was running at 939 and the intraday low till that time was 924.80, which was made at 9.30 during the day. In the above chart, you can clearly see the low level around 9.30, which is slightly below the previous close.

The intraday high was 940.45 at 11:10 am, so we had all the three data at 11:10 am as follows—

Previous Close = 925.70

Intraday High = 940.45

Intraday Low = 924.80

Now the average of these three is the pivot point, that is, if we add the above three and divide by 3, then we get 930.31. Now if the price is above this 930.31, then it is a bullish signal and if the price is below this 930.31, then it is a bearish signal.

Now when do we have to take a position in it?

See, there are 3 things in a pivot point. One is the previous close, which remains the same throughout the day, but the intraday high and intraday low can change during the day. On the basis of the intraday high of 940.45 formed at 11 am in the above chart, we knew at 11:10 am when the price was 939, that today the stock is in a bullish run, because the stock is still trading above its pivot point of 930.31.

Now we had to put a trigger order to buy at the intraday high of 940.25, that if the stock now comes above the intraday high of 940.25, we have to buy the stock.

In this way, if the stock was moving below the pivot point, we would know that today it is bearish and we could put a trigger order to do short selling at the intraday low.

In this, the target for intraday is kept equal to 1/4 of the value of π, i.e., 0.786 per cent.

In other words, you can see in the above chart that at around 11.50 am, the stock had made a new high at 940.50. You could have bought at that time and booked profit at 947.89, i.e., 0.786 per cent of 940.50 = 7.39, i.e., rupees 7.31 above 940.50.

Now you will ask what stop loss should be kept? Now I believe in telling you the method without stop loss, so after understanding the method of trading with pivot point and target, understand the method without stop loss.

In this regard, I will tell the story of a mango plant. Mr Ghasita planted a mango plant. It has soft pink leaves. Mr Ghasita waters it every day in the hope of getting mangoes; but when it does not yield mangoes for a month, Mr Ghasita uproots it and throws it away.

You will say, which fool's story have you started telling in the middle again? Actually, this is the story of an ordinary trader who suffers losses. In this method, you will have to first strengthen your mango tree, then you will eat mangoes.

To become a successful floor trader in this, follow the following steps:

1. Choose any 1-2-3 shares from the top 10 stocks with the highest market cap according to your capital.
2. A capital of ₹ 5 lakh for one stock is ideal. As I always say, intraday and future options are for full-time traders with high capital. So if you have a capital of ₹ 5 lakh, choose one stock, if you have a capital of ₹ 10 lakh, choose two shares and if you have a capital of ₹ 15 lakh, choose 3 shares.
3. Divide the capital into 50 parts, i.e., if you have a capital of ₹ 5 lakh, one part is of ₹ 10,000 (ten thousand).
4. In the initial days, place intraday orders only for buying.
5. Check the Pivot Point of the stock anytime between 10 am to 11.30 am. If the stock is trading above the Pivot Point, then in case of crossing the intraday high, place a buy order of one part of the capital, i.e., if it is ₹ 5 lakhs, then only ₹ 10,000. Keep the rest of the capital in some liquid ETF or you can use the rest of the capital in the 'Flow Method' which will be explained in the next chapter.

6. Leverage is available in intraday. Therefore, it is not that you have to take a position of ₹ 50,000 or ₹ 1,00,000 by investing ₹ 10,000. Whatever the margin may be of ₹ 1,000-2,000, you have to take a position of ₹ 10,000 only; because in this method, one has to take delivery if the trade goes against the trend. Hence, it is important to maintain sufficient cash.
7. If your order gets triggered due to intraday high, then earning a profit of 0.786 per cent is the ideal situation of this method. New traders should be satisfied if they get even 0.5 per cent after reducing brokerage and charges.
8. Now if you do not get the target after your order is triggered and the stock falls, then instead of booking a loss, take delivery.
9. There are approximately 248 trading sessions in a year, out of which you will get breakout on the basis of pivot point only in about 3 out of 5 days. In that too, only on 1 out of 3 days your trade will be likely to reverse without booking profit. Hence, it is assumed here that if you need to take delivery once in 5 trading sessions, then you have the capacity to take delivery up to 50 times, i.e., for almost the whole year.
10. Now, when you have taken delivery in some trades, then shares of the same company will start accumulating in your demat account at different prices.
11. If ever your stock is trading below the pivot point, then it is in the bearish zone. Now if the low of that day (which is made till you take the trade) is at least 0.786 per cent (approximately equal to 1/4 of the value of π) higher than the average price of the shares held in your demat, then you have earned the eligibility to short in intraday.
12. What I mean to say is that initially you use this method only on the buy side in intraday and take delivery when the trade goes against you. Now after taking some such delivery, even if your share comes in profit, you do not have to sell it. These shares held in demat will give you the eligibility to short sell in intraday at zero loss.

13. That is, suppose the average price of the shares with you in hold, which you have gradually collected in intraday when the trade goes against you, is 1,078.76. After that the stock came down to 1,127.30 but still you did not book profit. You just took trades using your pivot point system.
14. Now one day the stock is going bearish as per the Pivot Point system and the low of the day is 1,106.75 which is 2.59 per cent higher than your average price of 1,078.76. Now you place a short order at the trigger of the low of the day at 1,106.75 i.e., you short the stock below 1,106.75. So you have to cover your short position after getting a profit of 0.5 per cent after taking the ideal profit of 0.786 per cent and excluding brokerage.
15. If the trade goes in your favour then you have made a profit in intraday without selling even a single share of your demat account which is a good thing.
16. If the trade does not go in your favour and you had short sold at 1,106.75 and after that, if the stock rose further without falling much and closed at 1,145, did you incur a loss?
17. No. Just like you can take delivery for intraday purchase, you can give delivery on selling (short selling) if the shares are held in your demat account. That is, even if the stock comes to 1,145, if you choose the 'convert to delivery' option for your short position, then your shares will be considered sold at 1,106.75 and will be delivered from your demat account.
18. Now, at the price of 1,106.75, the stock is already at a profit of 2.59 per cent from your average price of 1,078.76. So, by giving delivery in this manner, you only made a profit of 2.59 per cent.
19. This means you have a win in both the hands. If the intraday trade goes in your favour then you will make a profit without selling any shares. If the intraday trade does not go in your favour then you will book a profit of 2.59 per cent on giving delivery.

20. The short trade position you have to take in this should not be equal to all the shares you hold, lest you come back to where you started in a single day.

21. Just as you had made the purchase in pieces of 10,000 each, even if you have shares worth ₹ 70,000 in your account, the said short trading should also be done for 10,000 only in a day, so that you can take trades in the same way in the coming days as well.

22. In this way, you have to develop a complete system in 1-2 or 3 blue chip shares as per your capital, in which you decide on long or short position on the basis of pivot point and take or give delivery if the trade is not in your favour.

23. You should consider yourself eligible to take a short position in this only when your held shares are in profit of at least 0.5 per cent or more than 0.786 per cent from the lowest level of that day (at which you are shorting).

So this was the complete system of trading on the basis of pivot point of some successful floor traders. How do you like this book? Have you got any benefit in your trading life from my hard work or not? If you express your views in this regard by reviewing the book on the related online platform from which you have bought the book, then I will be very happy to read your review.

❑

14

My Research on the Physics of the Stock Market

I have been working in the stock market since 2005. In these 19 years, I have invented many methods and researched on various methods of investing and trading.

On any holiday, I can be found doing various experiments in Excel sheets with stock market data on my laptop.

I also share the results of the research that I find exciting with you on my YouTube channel.

In my initial days in the stock market I preferred long- term investing and booked profit at a minimum of 15 per cent return. But I saw a significant decline in the market from its higher levels in 2008, 2011 and 2016. I found that in such declines, if we do not book profit in the bull run and wait for profit above 15 per cent, then many times the return that we have got is also lost. This is why I got inclined towards swing trading, in which it is very easy to earn a return of 4.50 per cent. In some research, I saw that on averaging, a return of 3 per cent is easily achieved.

Once in one of my research on compounding, I saw that if rupees 20000 are rotated by compounding by earning a profit of only 6 per cent, then in just 108 trades, it becomes more than rupees 1 crores.

In total, my mind kept revolving between 6 per cent, 4.50 per cent, 3 per cent. Similarly, in Darvas Box theory, I have seen that many times many purchases are made around the same price level. I saw that if a gap of at least 3 per cent is maintained between each purchase and the previous purchase, then unnecessary averaging can be avoided.

Similarly, I always found the best intraday profit target to be around 0.75 per cent. So, while doing research, I made its exact form 0.786 per cent instead of 0.75 in the Pivot Point method, which is equal to 1/4 of the value of Pi. It has been explained to you in the previous chapter.

To make quick money by buying ETFs during market downturns, I observed that buying some ETFs when the market falls by more than 1.50 per cent gives profit in the bounce back. This method has not been described in this book, as research on it is still going on. It will be described in future books or videos when it is completed.

Overall, I observed that there is an amazing similarity between 0.75 per cent, 1.50, 4.50 per cent and 6 per cent.

I kept on improving these points by back testing the past data. Finally I found that it fits best in the series 0.78, 1.57, 3.14, 4.71, 6.28.

All these values are related to the value of Pi a mathematical constant.

The value of π is equal to 22/7, i.e., approximately 3.14159.

Now if we divide pi by half, we get 1.57. 1/4 of π is related to my best intraday target of 0.78 per cent.

1.5 times of π is related to my best swing trading target of 4.71 per cent and 2 times of π is close to my target of 6.28 per cent for a little patient holding trade.

1/2 of π, i.e. 1.57, fits my ETF accumulate method on a fall.

Now π is a very mysterious mathematical constant. It is used in many formulae of mathematics and physics, the most famous of which is in finding the circumference of a circle.

Like a circle, the stock market is also cyclic. Bull and bear cycles keep coming in it too. My research is still in its initial stage, in which I am getting many proofs of the ups and downs of the stock market being related to π. It is possible that in the coming years, taking inspiration from this suggestion of mine, some technical indicator based on π may be invented.

Instead of hiding my knowledge, I believe in the principles of 'knowledge increases through sharing' and 'do good and good will happen'. That is why I have given you these initial hints. If you want, you can do further research on this.

Now, let me make you aware of some interesting facts about π.

In physics, the π constant is used in many formulae related to Earth, space and nature.

The ancient Babylonians considered the area of a circle to be 3 times the square of its radius, meaning they considered the value of π to be approximately 3.

An ancient Babylonian clay tablet gives the value of π as 3.125. Overall, π is an irrational number, with an infinite number of decimal places after 3. No one has been able to find its complete decimals. The Egyptian 'reed papyrus' states that the formula used by the Egyptians to find the area of a circle gave the value of π as 3.1605.

The English believe that the first correct value of pi was given by Archimedes. But the great Indian mathematician, Aryabhatta, gave an even more accurate value than Archimedes between 476 and 540 AD. He wrote in verse number 10 of 'Aryabhatiya Ganitapada'-

Chaturadhikam Shatamashtagunam
Dvashshistatha Sahasrana Aam.

Ayutdva yasya vishkambhasya
asannau vrittaparin aahh.

That is, in the case of a circle with a diameter of 20,000, multiply 104 by 8 and add to 62,000. Then on dividing the resulting number, 62,832, by 20,000, a constant is obtained, which is around 3.1416.

There is also a verse from the Mahabharata period in which Lord Krishna is praised. In this, the value of π was written in a code language so that it does not fall into the hands of others. In this, Lord Krishna is standing in the centre of a circle and the *gopis* are standing around the circumference of the circle and are reciting the following verse:

Gopibhagya madhuvrata: shrun gashodadhi sandhiga.

Khaljivitakh atav galhala rasandhar.

This verse is written in *Anushtup* stanza. If we decode it from the formula of the San s krit alphabet with the Katapayadi numbers, we get 3.14159, which is equivalent to the purest form of the value of pi. How is the Sanskrit alphabet decoded from the Katapayadi numbers? Since this is not the subject of this book, I am not giving the complete description. If you are interested in this, then search it on Google and get more information about it.

Overall, this lesson tells you the logic behind keeping the target 0.78, 1.57, 3.14, 4.71, 6.28 per cent. Along with this, you get to know the logic of keeping a gap of at least 3.14 per cent between two purchases in the Darvas Box method and the RSI method etc. My further research on this is continuing.

❑

15

Flow Method Based on Five-Day Low Price Level

This flow method is for the best management of the excess cash you have. By using it, you also get the benefit of the commodity market. I have already mentioned about it in my book *'Aap Bhi Ban Sakte Hain Intelligent Investor (You can also become an intelligent investor)'*. I have described this method in the present book for those who have not read the earlier-mentioned book. Also, since most of my methods mentioned in that book use only about 1/50th of the total capital, I have described this method in the present book with the objective of teaching them the method of management of excess cash.

Mutual Fund or ETF for Commodity Trading- Those who do not want to take the risk of futures and options for commodity trading can invest in it through Mutual Fund or Index Fund and ETF. In India, at present, ETF is available only for trading in gold and silver.

Diversification of Portfolio through Commodity Trading—

1. In this chapter, I will tell you my own tried and tested method of diversifying one's portfolio by investing in commodities through ETFs in cash instead of trading in commodities through futures and options. It is very important to have this diversity in the portfolio. I saw its direct benefit in the beginning of the year 2022 when the Russia-Ukraine war started. At that time, the prices of shares started falling badly. But gold-silver ETFs were giving good returns as the prices of gold and silver increased during the war. The same was

seen during the time of Corona, when the price of gold rose to an all-time high when the stock market fell. Even in the present time, i.e. in 2024, due to the Iran-Israel war, those who followed my method have got very good profits.

Therefore, by investing in gold and silver as per the method mentioned by me instead of cash in the portfolio, returns can be earned even on the cash which is lying unused.

Right now only gold and silver ETFs are available, in future; if ETFs of other commodities also come in the market then you can use this method in them also. I have named this method 'Flow Method' because with this, you will have cash flow even when the market falls.

Another reason for naming it 'Flow Method' is that it uses the lowest level (Low) formed in the last five days. Hence, the word 'Flow' has been formed by combining 'F' of five and 'low'. I myself also use this method for cash management. Although nothing can be safe in stock and commodity market, but this can be considered as the safest method; rest, the market risk will always remain.

First of all you have to decide how much you want to invest in this method in a year. I want to keep cash liquid of rupees 2 lakh to invest in the falling market, so that when the market falls, if I need up to rupees 2 lakh to buy new shares, then I can meet it from this ETF. You can decide as per your convenience how much you want to invest in this method in a year. Or you can use some part of the unused cash in Pivot Point etc. methods in this method.

Now if I want to invest in 2 ETFs for ₹ 2 lakh, then the potential investment per ETF is ₹ 1 lakh. Now if I divide ₹ 1 lakh in 52 weeks (there are approximately 52 weeks in a year), then the investment per week is approximately ₹ 1,923. Now in the flow method that I am going to tell you, you have to place 5 GTT or VTC orders in a trading week. GTT order means - Good Till Trigger Order and VTC order means - Valid Till Cancelled Order. Both the orders, once placed, remain valid for about a year; but we need the orders to remain valid for only five days. After five days, we will place new orders in place of those orders which are not triggered. In this, you have to place your GTT order on Saturday-Sunday, the market holidays, and leave it for the next week. For that, the lowest level of that ETF of the last five days of the market has to be taken. For example, the market was closed on Saturday and Sunday on 26th and 27th respectively. In this, if you have to place an order to buy Gold BeES (the ETF of gold which is traded in the highest volume) for the next trading week, then look at the prices of Gold BeES of the previous trading week.

Date	High level	Low level	Close price
21st March 2022	45.48	43.77	44.15
22nd March 2022	44.96	44.16	44.30
23rd March 2022	44.87	43.72	44.44
24th March 2022	45.27	44.38	44.59
25th March 2022	45.61	44.00	44.84

Now you have to place GTT orders for next week's purchase by reducing one paisa from the five lows formed in the last five days (last trading week) on 26th -27th March, 2022. How many shares (ETF units) are to be purchased in each order? We have to invest ₹ 1,923 per week and when you place five orders in this way by reducing one paisa from the lows of the last five days, then in the next week sometimes you will not get a single order triggered (if the price of gold rises) and sometimes only one of your five orders will get triggered and sometimes two-three can also get triggered and sometimes if there is a fall in the price of gold, then all your five orders will get triggered that week.

My experience is that on an average, you will have two orders getting triggered in a week. So if you want to invest ₹ 1,923 per month on an average, then it would be appropriate to put half of it, i.e. 961.50, in each order. That is, to the nearest integer, you have to place five buy orders of approximately ₹ 1,000 each by reducing the low of the last five days by one paisa. That is, on 26th and 27th March, you would have placed five buy orders of ₹ 1,000 each at the prices of 43.76, 44.15, 43.71, 44.37, 43.99 respectively. Now in the next trading week, the lows were made in the following manner—

Date	Low level
28th March 2022	44.27
29th March 2022	43.88
30th March 2022	43.88
31st March 2022	43.99
1st April 2022	43.15

This week, five of your five orders would have been triggered by the price going below the order. Now, new orders have to be filled, which would be four orders at 44.20, 43.87, 43.98, 43.14, one paisa below the previous week's low. Since the same low of 43.88 was made for two days last week, we have to fill only one order at 43.87, because there is no benefit in placing two orders at the same price.

In this system, you need a lot of patience and absolutely no greed; because when these five orders are placed, then due to the bull run of gold, its price went up to 46.32 on 19th April. Now when your average price of about 44 will be seen at 46, then you will feel that this is very interesting. You are getting 4-5 per cent in just 18 days, so you should increase your capital in it. But your thinking is wrong. If the price falls now, then even after your continuous orders are triggered, you will see a loss in your holding; but this loss may not be as much as in shares, but may be up to 5-10 per cent of your purchase average. But if you do not panic and close at that time, then gradually the average price will keep decreasing and when the price rises again, you will again get profit.

Therefore, you should neither increase your capital out of greed nor reduce it out of panic. Now you will say that what will happen, if there is a big fall in the price of gold and silver and the price does not rise again for 15-20 years; then what will I do? If this happens, then the value of the jewellery lying in your house will also decrease. Then you can sell these ETFs and get jewellery made in return, which your wife will wear and you will leave behind gold and silver as inheritance for your generations.

Also, remember that if this happens, then those who use other methods of investing in gold and silver will incur more losses than you. Since you are buying a little bit at lower than the daily lows, your average cost will always be low and if everything goes well and you have invested around ₹ 1 lakh in 52 weeks, then you will see that your investment will often be in 5-10-15 per cent profit and when you need cash when the stock market falls, you will be able to book profit in it and buy shares in the fall.

For those readers who want to trade in it, there is a very simple method that whenever the average price is giving you more than 3.14 per cent return, then book profit and keep running the system further. Those who do not want to do many trades can book profit of 6.28 per cent. Another way is that you let the system run and whenever you need cash, sell only that amount of ETF.

Overall, I consider this method to be the safest and most profitable in commodity, the rest is speculation and in speculation, there are more losses in pursuit of more profit.

To make gold and silver jewellery, one has to work very hard with a small hammer. Only then, attractive jewellery is made, which is used on auspicious occasions as an inheritance for generations. But it takes only a few hits with a big hammer to make a sharp sword of iron. So you have to decide whether you want to walk on the edge of the sword by investing a big amount (big hammer) in futures and options or you want to walk slowly with my method.

You can gradually invest the remaining ₹ 1 lakh in Silver ETF using the above method. Here another question will arise. To understand it, look at the data of Silver ETF and Gold BeES for the following 5 dates. In the trading week of 18th April to 22nd April, 2022, the prices of NETF SILVER were as follows-

Date	High price	Low price	Close price
18th April 2022	69.99	68.31	69.61
19th April 2022	69.98	69.31	69.88
20th April 2022	69.18	67.86	68.00
21st April 2022	68.20	67.35	67.40
22nd April 2022	67.83	66.15	66.30

Now, since the market is closed on 23rd and 24th April, 2022 due to holiday on Saturday-Sunday, and we have to place orders to buy NETF

SILVER for the next trading week, then as per the rule, we should place buy orders of ₹ 1,000 each at the low level of the five trading days of the previous week, i.e. 68.31, 69.31, 67.86, 67.35 and 66.15. But here the closing price of NETF SILVER on 22nd April, 2022 is 66.30, which is less than all the four – 68.31, 69.31, 67.86 and 67.35.

When the closing price at the time of placing the order is 66.30, then there is no justification in placing a buy order at a price above this. So in such a situation, we have to place only one order at 66.15, because 66.15 is the only lowest level of the previous week, which is lower than the close price of 66.30 at the end of the week.

Now you will ask, should we buy only for ₹ 1,000 at 66.15 or should we place an order of 5,000 by including the amount of the remaining part of the order in it? The answer to this is that you have to place an order of only one part, that is, 1,000 at 66.15, because this type of situation indicates that the silver market is in a bear phase and its price can fall further. So in such a situation we have to place only one order of ₹ 1,000 at 66.15, the remaining amount will be used in the coming weeks. Similarly, the prices of Gold BeES from 18th April, 2022 to 22nd April, 2022 were also as follows—

Date	High price	Low price	Close price
18th April 2022	46.29	45.80	45.73
19th April 2022	46.32	45.63	46.19
20th April 2022	47.49	44.93	45.98
21st April 2022	47.60	45.09	45.22
22nd April 2022	45.84	45.08	45.21

In this also, the two-day lows of 45.80 and 45.63 are higher than the last close price of 45.21 and only 3 levels, 44.93, 45.09, 45.08, are suitable for filling quotes for buying. In this also you will see that 45.09 and 45.08 are very close levels, with a difference of only rupees 0.01.

Hence, if the difference between the two lowest levels is less than rupees 0.10, then they should also be ignored and next week, only two

GTT orders of 44.92, by reducing 1 paisa from 44.93, and 45.08, by reducing 1 paisa from 45.09, should be filled.

Therefore, as ETFs of only two commodities, gold and silver, are available at present, you can gradually collect units in them using the above method and whenever you get more than 8 per cent profit from the average price, you can book profit at that time or keep them in your account instead of cash and when the market falls, you can sell shares and buy more shares.

❑

16

Summary of Trading with Price Action Breakout

Price action trading is a method that focuses on the market movement and decisions are made based only on the price chart. It does not require any external indicators like RSI, MACD or moving averages. Breakout trading is one of the most popular methods of price action trading that involves the price breaking above or below a certain level. In this article, we will understand in detail how to trade with price action breakout and what are the key points to keep in mind in order to implement it successfully.

1. What is Price Action Trading?

Price action trading is a purely chart-based strategy that takes trading decisions by studying the candlesticks and price movement on the chart. It does not use external factors such as news, economic data or other technical indicators. Traders simply identify trades and important levels based on price and time to look for buying or selling opportunities.

Some of the key features of price action trading are:

- **Simplicity:** This method is very simple as compared to indicator-based strategies, which only requires attention to the charts and candlesticks.
- **Accuracy:** Price action strategy allows you to closely observe market fluctuations and make quick decisions accordingly.
- **Flexibility:** This strategy can be used in any type of market, such as stock market, forex or commodity.

2. What is a Breakout?

A breakout is a situation when the price moves in a new direction after crossing a specific level, such as support or resistance. This often happens when there is imbalance in the market and either buyers or sellers have a clear edge.

Major types of Breakouts -

- **Upside Breakout:** When the price crosses a resistance level and moves upwards.
- **Downside Breakout:** When the price breaks a support level and falls downwards.

3. Breakout Trading Strategies

3.1. Identifying Support and Resistance Levels

The first and most important step in breakout trading is to identify the correct support and resistance levels on the chart. These are the key levels where the price frequently pauses or reverses. As soon as the price breaks these levels, it is likely to move rapidly in a new direction. In this book, I have already devoted an entire chapter to explain trading based on support and resistance.

3.2. Identifying Consolidation Patterns

Consolidation is an important indicator in breakout trading. Consolidation represents the time when there is a struggle between buyers and sellers in the market and the price keeps moving in a limited range. After this phase, a sharp change is seen in the price and this change often comes in the form of a breakout. You have already understood its description in the chapter on consolidated breakout.

3.3. Volume Analysis

Volume analysis is very important to confirm a breakout. When the price breaks a support or resistance level, high volume is a reliable indicator that the breakout is genuine. If the volume is low at the time of the breakout, it may be a false breakout, in which the price may return in the range.

3.4. Avoiding False Breakouts

Many times the price immediately retraces back into the range after breaking a support or resistance level. This is called a 'false breakout' and to avoid this you should wait for confirmation signals. Using volume, candlestick patterns and other chart indicators, you can differentiate between a genuine breakout and a false breakout.

4. Important Chart Patterns for Breakouts

4.1. Triangle Pattern

Ascending Triangle: This pattern shows the possibility of an upside breakout. In this, the price forms higher lows and finally breaks a strong resistance.

The Ascending Triangle pattern is a bullish continuation pattern, which is used in technical analysis. This pattern shows that the demand (buyers) in the market is gradually increasing, while the supply (sellers) remains stable. The structure of this pattern is as follows—

- **Horizontal Resistance Line (Upper Limit):** The price repeatedly tests a certain level, but is unable to go above that level. This level is called 'resistance' and it forms a horizontal line.
- **Rising Support Line (Lower Limit):** A rising trend line is formed every time the price makes a higher low instead of a lower low. This trend line indicates strength of the buyers.
- **Breakout** - When the price breaks out above the resistance line, it indicates that the buyers have defeated the sellers and the chances of a sharp rise in price increase. The horizontal line above represents the resistance level.

The diagonal line below represents the support level, which is moving upwards.

Key Points —

- **Volume:** It is important for the volume to increase at the time of breakout. This confirms that the breakout is genuine.
- **Target Price:** The target of the expected price movement after the breakout can be determined. For this, the distance between the

highest and lowest points of the triangle is measured and projected from the breakout point. A hypothetical diagram of this is given below.

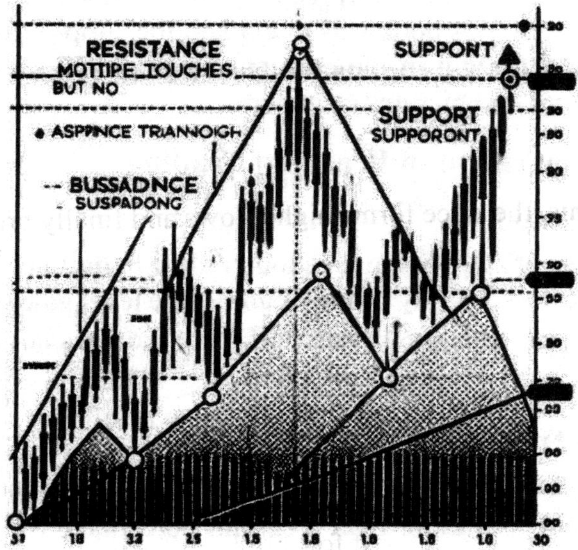

Ascending Triangle Imaginary Image (AI generated)

If you see this pattern in a real chart, it may indicate a bullish trend continuation.

- **Descending Triangle:** This pattern indicates a downside breakout, where the price makes lower highs and eventually breaks a strong support.

4.2. Flag and Pennant Patterns

- **Flag Pattern:** The flag pattern represents a brief consolidation after a bullish trend, which may mark the start of a new trend in the market. When the price breaks out of the flag pattern, it may signal a significant breakout.
- **Pennant Pattern:** This is similar to the flag, but the consolidation is in the form of a narrowing triangle. When the price breaks out of the pennant, it may confirm a new trend.

I have included the names and facts of all the above patterns for your general information, so that you can guess how you would have liked this book if I had written it by showing the names and pictures of the patterns in this way instead of describing the practical methods. But whatever methods I have told you in this book on the basis of my own research, if you see them on the chart, you will see similar patterns. Therefore, do not get too confused with such names and pictures. My purpose of writing this book was to explain the simplest forms of price action breakout trading in the current context without confusing you with such names and pictures of patterns.

5. Risk Management in Breakout Trading

5.1. Use of Stop Loss

The correct use of stop loss in breakout trading helps in controlling your risk. Set a stop loss slightly below or above the level where the breakout occurred. This will limit your losses if the price does not move in your direction.

5.2. Proper Trade Size

Always choose the proper trade size. For risk-management it is essential that you do not lose more than a certain percentage of your account. This rule helps you protect yourself from potential losses and allows you to hold for a longer period of time.

5.3. Trailing the Trade after the Breakout

As soon as the price starts moving in your favour, you can trail your stop loss behind the price. This will help you secure potential profits and avoid any unexpected reversal in the market.

6. Mental Discipline and Patience

Mental discipline and patience are very important in price action breakout trading. Always wait for the right opportunities in the market and be careful to avoid false breakouts. Avoid being in a hurry in the market and always act according to your trading plan.

7. Advantages of Price Action Breakout Trading

7.1. Clear and Precise Signals

Price action breakout trading gives you clear and precise trading signals. This makes this strategy easy to understand and implement.

7.2. High Profit Opportunities

When the market breaks out, it can be a sign of a strong trend in a new direction. Such trades provide you with opportunities to make faster and higher profits.

7.3. Flexible Use

This strategy can be applied to any market, be it stocks, forex or commodities. Moreover, you can use it on any timeframe.

Conclusion

Price action breakout trading is a powerful technique that can be extremely profitable for traders if used correctly. Successful breakout trading requires you to identify market support and resistance levels, analyse volumes, and follow risk-management measures. However, this technique requires patience and discipline, as the market does not always move as expected.

The previous chapters of this book have explained to you the simplest way to use these price action breakout techniques without a chart. With the right planning and mental discipline, you can successfully apply the strategies described in the book to your trading career.

❑

17

Confusion of Technical Analysis

This is the last chapter of this book. You can also consider it as a conclusion of the book in a way.

There are many indicators of technical analysis in the world and the common trader keeps wandering from one indicator to another in search of an indicator with 100 per cent success.

Always remember that the uncertainty of the stock market is its biggest characteristic. You cannot trade with 100 per cent success with any method and any indicator of the stock market.

It is also the case in the stock market that one indicator will give you a bullish signal and the other indicator will give you a bearish signal.

When you feel that the market is going to rise, then the market will fall and when you are sure about the fall of the market, then the market will surprise you by rising.

So, the bottom line is that keep in mind the quote of a famous saint –

Keep shedding blood and sweat,
Keep sleeping with the sheet pulled tight.
This boat will keep on moving,
Whether you keep laughing or crying.

Meaning, just like the boat of life has many ups and downs, similarly the stock market also has its ups and downs.

So that we can go into this market laughing and sleeping with the sheet pulled over our head, always keep these things in mind -

1. Do not associate the stock market with your ego.
2. Do not mix many methods and technical indicators together. The most important thing is to work continuously with discipline in all the methods.
3. Do not make big investments out of greed, because nothing is guaranteed here.
4. Never invest your parents' money or your spouse's money or borrowed money.
5. Keep another regular source of income and make it a habit to save 10 per cent of that income regularly and invest regularly at every level of the market.
6. Always use the methods of this book in good and established companies, so that you do not need to keep a stop loss like me.
7. Divide your capital into at least 50 parts for each method and invest only one part at a time.
8. Control your emotions and do not rush in the stock market. Do not consider it a game but a business for life.

I or my family members may have invested in all the companies mentioned in the book. This book is for educational purpose only. Do not consider it as investment advice and before investing or using any method, do your own research and act according to your discretion and your risk-taking capacity.

I, the author of this book, will not be responsible for any loss. Please do not contact me personally on phone or email for guidance. Due to having millions of followers, I am unable to guide everyone personally. All my services are free. Therefore, do not make any payment to any scammer in my name. Also, please do not try to meet me by visiting my home without informing me, because I find this inconvenient due to having lakhs of followers. Thank you!

I bow to the divine element residing in all your hearts and express my gratitude to that supreme power for making me a medium for getting this book written. I request all of you to definitely review this book, so that I can know whether my hard work of years have been useful for you or not!

With the wish of the well-being of all, I thank God and end the writing of this book here.

—Mahesh Chandra Kaushik

SEBI Registered Research Analyst

❑